CONGREVE'S COMEDY OF MANNERS

Borgo Press Books by FRANK J. MORLOCK

Chuzzlewit
Congreve's Comedy of Manners
Crime and Punishment
Falstaff (with William Shakespeare, John Dennis, and William Kendrick)
Fathers and Sons
The Idiot
Jurgen
Justine
Lord Jim
Notes from the Underground
Oblomov
Outrageous Women: Lady Macbeth and Other French Plays (editor and translator)
Peter and Alexis
The Princess Casamassima
A Raw Youth
The Stendhal Hamlet Scenarios and Other Shakespearean Shorts from the French (editor and translator)

CONGREVE'S COMEDY OF MANNERS

A PLAY IN FIVE ACTS

FRANK J. MORLOCK

Adapted from the Plays by William Congreve

THE BORGO PRESS
MMXII

CONGREVE'S COMEDY OF MANNERS

Copyright © 1982, 2012 by Frank J. Morlock

FIRST BORGO PRESS EDITION

Published by Wildside Press LLC

www.wildsidebooks.com

DEDICATION

*For Carmen Martínez,
who would make a great Angelica*

CONTENTS

INTRODUCTION 9
CAST OF CHARACTERS. 11
ACT I, Scene 1 13
ACT I, Scene 2 45
ACT I, Scene 3 61
ACT II, Scene 4. 63
ACT III, Scene 5 91
ACT III, Scene 6 121
ACT IV, Scene 7 143
ACT IV, Scene 8 157
ACT IV, Scene 9 171
ACT IV, Scene 10. 191
ACT V, Scene 11 201
ACT V, Scene 12 209
ACT V, Scene 13 217
ABOUT THE AUTHOR 225

INTRODUCTION

My intention in writing this play was to distill the essence of Congreve, to the extent of my ability, into one stage-worthy play. Congreve wrote four comedies, *The Way of The World* being his acknowledged masterpiece. *Love for Love* is less brilliant but easier to perform, though it seldom is. His earlier plays, *The Old Bachelor* and the *Double Dealer*, contain very good material but are rarely read let alone performed. Revival is unlikely. I had the idea of building a pastiche of all the comedies.

My plan was to build on the general plot of *Love for Love*, and weave characters and dialogue from the other plays into and around it. In the process some characters are blended with other characters, and acquire clever dialogue found elsewhere. The result is, hopefully, a lively play that will keep Congreve's best work before the public eye.

But for a transitional phrase or two, almost every line in this play is Congreve's. It stands to reason then, that whatever virtues it has are his, and whatever faults are mine. The play is not meant as an imitation or improvement of Congreve but rather a "good parts" version of his existing works.

—Frank J. Morlock

CAST OF CHARACTERS

Men

Foresight, an astrologer

Sir Sampson Plyant, a crusty old man

Valentine, his son, in love with Angelica

Ben, his younger son, a naval officer

Lord Froth, an exquisite gentleman

Scandal, Valentine's friend

Maskwell, a villain, secretary to Foresight

Tattle, a beau valued for his secrecy

Women

Lady Foresight, an adulterous wife in love with Valentine

Angelica, a spirited and affected young woman, niece

to Foresight

Mrs. Frail, sister to Foresight, a woman of the town

Prue, Foresight's daughter by an earlier marriage

Nurse

Servant

The drama is set in London, circa 1699.

ACT I
SCENE 1

A room in Foresight's house. The room is furnished with various astrological paraphernalia. Foresight, a fiftyish, pedantic man in a rather unstylish wig, enters and addresses an old servant woman.

Foresight

What, are all the women in my family abroad? Is not my wife come home? Nor my sister, nor my daughter?

Servant

No, sir.

Foresight

What can be the meaning of it? Sure the moon is in all her fortitudes. Is my niece Angelica at home?

Servant

Yes, sir.

Foresight

I believe you lie, madame.

Servant

Sir?

Foresight

I say you lie. It is impossible that anything should be as I would have it; for I was born when the Crab was ascendant and all my affairs go backward.

Servant

I can't tell, indeed, sir.

Foresight

No, I know you can't, madame. But I can tell, and foretell, too.

Servant

Ha, ha, ha.

Foresight

What's the matter?

Servant

You have put on one stocking inside out.

Foresight

That may be a sign of very good luck. I have had several omens recently. I got out of bed backwards this morning—and without premeditation—pretty good that—but then a black cat crossed my path —bad that. Some bad, some good. (looking at his watch) Three o'clock. A very good hour for business.

(Enter Angelica.)

Angelica

Is it not a good hour for pleasure too, Uncle Foresight? Pray lend me your coach, mine's out of order.

Foresight

What, would you be gadding about, too? Sure all these females are mad today. An evil portent. I remember a prophecy—it bodes of cuckoldom.

Angelica

But Uncle Foresight, I can neither make you a cuckold by going out, nor secure you from it by staying at home.

Foresight

Not so. While one woman is left in the house, the prophecy is not in full force—

Angelica

But my inclinations are in force; I have a mind to go out. If you won't lend me your coach, I'll take a hackney. Cast a horoscope and see who is in conjunction with your wife. You know my Aunt is a little retrograde in her nature. I'm afraid you are not the lord of the ascendant. Ha, ha, ha.

Foresight

You are a very pert flirt.

Angelica (stifling her laughter)

Uncle, don't be angry. If you are, I'll swear you are a nuisance to the neighborhood with your false prophecies, miraculous dreams, and idle divinations.

Foresight

Why, you malapert—

Angelica

Will you lend me your coach? Or I'll continue: Nay, I'll declare how your prophesized popery was coming.

Indeed, Uncle, I'll indict you for a wizard.

Foresight

Was there ever such a provoking minx?

Servant

How she talks—

Angelica

Yes, and I can make oath of your unlawful midnight practices, you and old Nanny there.

Servant

Oh, Lord, I at midnight practices!

Angelica

Yes. I saw you two together through the keyhole one night, like Satan and the Witch of Endor pricking your thumbs to write poor innocents' names in blood.

Foresight

I defy you, hussy.

Angelica

I know something worse, if I would speak of it.

Foresight

I'll remember this; I'll be revenged on you, cockatrice; I'll hamper you. You have your fortune in your own hands, but—

Angelica

Will you? All shall out then. Look to it, Nanny. I can bear witness that you have a great unnatural teat under your left arm and he another, and that you suckle a young devil in the shape of a tabby cat, by turns—I can.

Foresight

A teat. A teat. I, an unnatural teat! Oh, false slanderous thing.

Servant (pushing her bust out)

Feel, feel here if I have anything but what is like any other Christian.

Foresight

I will have patience. It is in my stars that I should be thus tormented. This is the effect of the malicious conjunctions and oppositions in the third house of my nativity; there the curse of kindred was foretold. But I'll punish you. I'll have my doors locked up. Not one man, not one gallant shall enter my house. Consider that, hussy.

Angelica

Do, Uncle, do. Lock 'em up quickly before my Aunt comes home. You'll have a letter for alimony tomorrow morning. But let me begone first, and then let no man come near this house but he who converses with spirits and the celestial signs, the bull, and the ram, and the goat. Bless me! There are a great many horned beasts among the twelve signs. But patient cuckolds, they say, go to heaven.

Foresight

There's but one virgin among the twelve signs, spitfire, but one virgin.

Angelica

No doubt she had an astrologer husband. That is what makes my Aunt go abroad.

Foresight

How? How? Is that the reason? Come, you know something. Tell me, and I'll forgive you. Do, good Niece. Come, you shall have my coach and horses. Does my wife complain? I know women tell one another—she has a wanton eye and was born under Gemini, which may incline her to—incline; she has a mole upon her lip and a moist palm, and an open liberality on the mount of Venus—

Angelica

Ha, ha, ha.

Foresight

Don't perplex your poor Uncle. Tell me. Won't you speak?

Angelica

Goodbye, Uncle. Ha, ha, ha. I'll find out my Aunt and tell her she must not come home.

(Enter Valentine, a magnificent Chevalier, who bows deeply to Angelica.)

Angelica

Ah, Valentine, you here?

Foresight

Ha, your gallant has arrived. We'll speak of this another time, Niece. Come, Nurse.

(Foresight and Nurse go out.)

Angelica

Valentine, did you take exception last night? Oh, aye—and went away. Now I think on it, I am angry. No, now I think on it, I am pleased, for I believe I gave you some pain.

Valentine

Does that please you?

Angelica

Infinitely! I love to give pain.

Valentine

Do not affect cruelty. Your true nature is the power of pleasing.

Angelica

Oh, I ask your pardon for that. One's cruelty is one's power, and when one parts with one's cruelty, one parts with one's power and when one parts with that, I fancy one's old and ugly.

Valentine

To be sure, sacrifice your lover to your cruelty. But I'll tell you a secret: beauty is a lover's gift, it is a reflection of a lover's praise, not a woman's face.

Angelica

By which you prove that if I give up my lover, I give up my beauty? Vain man. You would never have loved me if I were not handsome. Why, one makes lovers as fast as one pleases and they live as long as one pleases, and they die as soon as one pleases, and if one pleases one makes more.

Valentine

Very pretty.

Angelica

I'd as soon owe my beauty to a lover as my wit to an echo.

Valentine

Ah, but you do.

Angelica

How so?

Valentine

To your lover, you owe the pleasure of hearing yourself praised, and to an echo, the pleasure of hearing yourself talk.

Angelica

Fah! I'm going out.

Valentine

I would beg a little private audience. You had the tyranny to deny me last night, though I came to impart a secret that concerned our love.

Angelica

You saw I was engaged.

Valentine

You had the leisure to entertain a herd of fools. How can you delight in such society?

Angelica

I please myself—besides, I do it for my health.

Valentine

Your health!

Angelica

Yes. It prevents the vapors. If you persist in this offensive freedom, you'll displease me. I think I must resolve, after all, not to have you. We shan't agree.

Valentine

Not as regards medicinal matters.

Angelica

And yet, our distemper shall be the same, for we shall be sick of one another. I shan't endure to be reprimanded, nor instructed; 'tis so tedious to be told one's faults. I can't bear it. Well, I won't have you, Valentine. I'm resolved. (hesitating) I think— You may go. (bursts out laughing) Ha, ha, ha. (Valentine shows signs of being thoroughly vexed) (good-naturedly, almost mischievously) What would you give that you could help loving me?

Valentine (furious)

I would give something if you did not know I cannot help it!

Angelica

Come, don't look so grave then—it's a sure sign.

Valentine

A man may as soon make a friend with his wit or a fortune by his honesty as win a woman with sincerity!

Angelica

Sententious Valentine! Prithee, don't look so wise and violent—like Solomon at the dividing of the child.

Valentine (controlling himself)

You are a merry madame, but I would persuade you to be serious for a moment.

Angelica

What, with that face? No, if you keep your countenance it is impossible I should keep mine. (musing) Well, after all, there is something very moving in a lovesick face. Ha, ha, ha. Well, I won't laugh, it would be cruel—don't be peevish. Ah, now I'll be melancholy, as melancholy as, as a poet. (she assumes a very melancholy pose) Well, Val, if you ever would win me, woo me now. (Valentine remains furiously silent) Ah, if you are so tedious, fare you well— (starts to leave)

Valentine

Can you not find in the variety of your disposition even one moment?

Angelica

To hear you tell me that your father proposes to disinherit you?

Valentine

But, how came you to know of it?

Angelica

I will leave you to consider. When you have done thinking of that, think of me.

(Angelica sails out, leaving Valentine perplexed and cursing under his breath.)

Valentine (exploding)

INCONSTANT CREATURE!

(That stops Angelica and she returns.)

Angelica

You can't accuse me of inconstancy; I never told you that I love you.

Valentine

Then I accuse you of not telling me whether you do or not.

Angelica

I have never troubled myself to make up my mind on the question.

Valentine

Nor good nature enough to do so—

Angelica

What, are you setting up for good nature?

Valentine

As women do for virtue, for the affectation of it. (desperately) Why won't you hear me with patience?

Angelica

I'm tired of being pestered with flames and stuff. I think I shan't endure the sight of a fire this twelvemonth.

Valentine

Even fire cannot melt that cruel, frozen heart.

Angelica

God, how I hate your hideous fancy; if you must talk of love, for heaven's sake, do it with variety; don't always come like the devil wrapped up in flames. I'll not hear another sentence that begins: "I burn...."

Valentine

Tell me how you would be adored. I am very tractable.

Angelica

In silence.

Valentine

Humph, I thought so, that you might have all the talk to yourself—you had better let me speak, or I'll make villainous signs—

Angelica

What would you get by that? I won't understand signs.

Valentine

If I am to be tongue-tied, my actions will quicken your apprehensions and—egad—let me tell you my most prevailing argument is expressed in dumb show.

Angelica

Foh! An ape is a more troublesome thing than a parrot.

Valentine

There are few men but do more silly things than they say. Faith, I could be well pleased to drive a bargain in silence—it would save a man a world of swearing and lying. When wit and reason both have failed to move, Kind looks and actions from success do prove.

Angelica

Your father is coming, and I'm leaving.

(Angelica exits; Sir Sampson Plyant, Valentine's father, enters with Foresight.)

Valentine

Your blessing, sir.

Sampson

You've had it already today, sir. I think I sent it to you in a bill for four thousand pounds. If there was too much, refund the superfluity, dost hear, Boy?

Valentine

Superfluity! Sir, it will scarcely pay my debts.

Sampson

Indeed. Then you should have less of them.

Valentine

I hope you will not hold me to the hard conditions I

agreed to—

Sampson

Here's a rogue, Brother Foresight, makes a bargain in the morning and would be released in the afternoon. Here's honesty; here's conscience.

Valentine

The bargain was made under duress.

Sampson

I shall hold you to it to the letter. Do you deny it?

Valentine

I don't deny it, Father.

Sampson

Dog, you'll be hanged. I shall live to see you go to Tyburn. Has he not a rogue's face? Speak, Brother, you understand physiognomy—a hanging look to me.

Foresight (not unkindly)

Hmmm—truly, I don't care to discourage a young man—he has madness in his face—but, I see no danger of hanging—

Valentine (aside)

Madness. There's a lucky thought. (aloud) Sir, this usage to your Son will drive me mad.

Sampson

Why, who are you, sir?

Valentine

Your son, sir.

Sampson

That's more than I know, sir, and I believe not.

Valentine

Indeed. Then, I hope I am not.

Sampson

What, would you make your mother a whore! (to Foresight) Did you ever hear the like?

Valentine

I was merely offering an excuse for your barbarity.

Sampson

Excuse! Why, may I not do as I please? Did you come a

volunteer into this world or did I press you into service, eh?

Valentine

I know no more why I came than you do. But I came with all the appetites and senses that you begot along with me.

Sampson

Oons, what had I to do to get children? He must have appetites! Why, you'd rather eat pheasant than mutton and drink wine rather than beer. And smell. I warrant he can smell and loves perfumes above a stench. Why, there it is. And music. Don't you love music, scoundrel?

Valentine

I'm told I have a good ear—

Sampson

A good ear! If this rogue were dissected, I'll warrant he has vessels of digestion large enough for a Cardinal. Oons, if I had that four thousand pounds again I would not give you one shilling. 'Sheart, you were always fond of wit. Now, let's see if you can live by your wit. Your brother will be in town today, then look to your covenant—you must renounce all title to your estate in his favor.

Valentine

I have agreed to it, Father. But I think it very harsh. Good day, sir.

(Valentine bows and goes out.)

Sampson

No more to be said, Old Merlin, that's plain. Here it is. (brandishing a paper) I have it in my hand, Old Ptolemy. He thought if he danced until doomsday, I was to pay the piper. Well, here it is, under seal.

Foresight

What is it, anyway?

Sampson

In return for saving that spendthrift from prison for debt, I have made him agree to renounce his inheritance in favor of his brother Ben. Body oh me, I'm so glad to be revenged on this unnatural rogue.

Foresight

Let me see—so it is. When was this signed? You should have consulted me as to the time.

Sampson

No matter for the time. It's signed.

Foresight

But the time is all important.

Sampson

Brother Foresight, leave superstition. Pox on the time. There's no time like the present.

Foresight

You are very ignorant.

Sampson

If the sun shine by day and the stars by night—why, we shall know one another without the help of a candle—and that's all the stars are good for.

Foresight

How, how? Give me leave to contradict you. You are an ignorant agnostic and skeptic.

Sampson

Ignorant! Why, I have traveled the globe and seen the antipodes where the sun rises at midnight and sets at noon.

Foresight

But I can tell you that I have traveled in the celestial spheres, known the signs and the planets and their houses. Can judge of motions, direct and retrograde. Know whether life shall be long or short, happy or unhappy, if journeys shall be prosperous, undertakings successful, or stolen goods recovered. Furthermore, I know—

Sampson

And I know the length of the Emperor of China's foot! And I have made a cuckold of a king. Body oh me, the present Majesty of Bantam is the issue of these loins!

Foresight

I know when braggarts lie or speak the truth, even when they don't know it themselves.

Sampson

I have known an astrologer made a cuckold in the twinkling of a star; and seen a conjuror that could not keep the devil out of his wife's circle—ha, Old Wizard. Old Galileo.

Foresight

Do you mean my wife, Sir Sampson? By the body of the sun—

Sampson

By the horns of the moon, you would say, Brother Capricorn.

Foresight

Capricorn in your teeth, Liar. Take back your inheritance and put your son Ben back to sea. I'll wed my daughter Prue to an Egyptian mummy before she shall incorporate with the son of one who scoffs at science.

Sampson

Body oh me, I have gone too far. I must not provoke Copernicus too much. An Egyptian mummy is an illustrious creature, my trusty hieroglyphic, and may have significations about him. What, thou art not angry for a jest, my Good Kepler. I would Ben were an Egyptian mummy for your sake. I reverence the sun, the moon, and the stars with all my heart.

Foresight

Well, why didn't you say so?

Sampson

I love to jest. Now I think on it, I have the foot of an Egyptian mummy that I purloined from one of the pyramids when I was last in Egypt having an affair with the Pasha's wife. You shall have it.

Foresight

But, what do you know of my wife, Sir Sampson?

Sampson

Your wife is a constellation of virtues; she's the moon and you are the man in the moon. I was but in jest. (aside) A more shameless whore never lived.

(Sir Sampson and Foresight exit. Enter Mrs. Frail and Lady Froth at another door.)

Mrs. Frail

Indeed, madame! Is it possible your ladyship was so much in love?

Lady Froth

I could not sleep; I did not sleep for three weeks together.

Mrs. Frail

Prodigious! I wonder, want of sleep and so much love, and so much wit, as your ladyship has did not turn your brain.

Lady Froth

Oh, my dear Frail, you must tease your friend. But really, I wonder too. But I had a way. For between you and I, I had whimsies and vapors but I gave them vent.

Mrs. Frail

How?

Lady Froth

Oh, I writ, writ abundantly. Do you never write?

Mrs. Frail

Write what?

Lady Froth

Songs, elegies, satires, panegyrics, lampoons, plays and heroic poems.

Mrs. Frail

Oh Lord, not I.

Lady Froth

Oh, inconsistent, in love and not write! If my lord and I had been both of your temper, we had not come together. Bless me, what a sad thing that would have been.

Mrs. Frail

Then neither of you would ever have met with your match.

Lady Froth

Very true. I think he wants nothing but a blue ribbon and a star to make him shine the very phosphorus of our hemisphere. Do you understand those hard words? If no, I'll explain them to you.

Mrs. Frail.

Yes, yes, I'm not so ignorant. (aside) At least I won't own it to be troubled with your instruction.

Lady Froth

But I'm amazed you don't write. How can your amant believe you love him?

Mrs. Frail

Oh, I have a way of showing him that leaves no doubt.

But, Lady Froth, you must see my new dress. I had it brought from Paris.

Lady Froth

I shall be delighted. But, you really don't write?

(They go out. Enter Lady Foresight at another door, followed by Maskwell. Lady Foresight is an aging, but still beautiful woman. At the moment she is in a rage. Maskwell is trying to placate her.)

Lady Foresight

I'll hear no more. You are false and ungrateful. Come, I know you are false.

Maskwell

I have been frail in your ladyship's service—

Lady Foresight

That I should trust a man who had betrayed his friend—

Maskwell

What friend have I betrayed or to whom?

Lady Foresight

Valentine—and to me. Can you deny it?

Maskwell

I do not.

Lady Foresight

And have you not wronged my husband? And in the highest manner—in his bed?

Maskwell

With your ladyship's help and assistance. I can't deny that either. Anything more, madame?

Lady Foresight

More! Have you not dishonored me?

Maskwell

No, that I deny; for I never told a soul. So that accusation is answered. On to the next, for I see you have more.

Lady Foresight

Insolent devil! Do you mock my passion? Have a care! One word to my husband and you are ruined.

Maskwell

Will you be in a temper, madame? I would not talk to

be heard. I have been a very great rogue for your sake, and you reproach me with it; I am ready to be a rogue still to do you service. And you fling conscience and honor in my face. How am I to behave?

Lady Foresight

Impudent villain. Do you dare to say this to me?

Maskwell (icily)

Look you, madame, we are alone. Contain yourself and hear me. You know you loved Valentine when I first sighed for you—but you only favored my passion through revenge and policy.

Lady Foresight

Liar! Have I not met your love with passion?

Maskwell

Only to aid your revenge on Valentine. To entice me, that I might betray him to you.

Lady Foresight

Damnation! Do you provoke me again?

Maskwell

Nay, madame, I'm gone if you relapse. I say nothing

but what you yourself have confessed to me. Why should you deny it? How can you?

(Lady Foresight walks about in a fury, fanning herself.)

Maskwell

I am your slave—the slave of all your pleasures. I will prevent his marriage to Angelica.

Lady Foresight

Oh, Maskwell, in vain do I disguise myself before you—you know me—to the very inmost windings of my soul.

Maskwell

Compose yourself. You shall possess and ruin him, too. Will that please you?

Lady Foresight

How, how? You dear, you precious villain, how? Let him once be mine and immediate ruin seize him the next!

Maskwell

His father has forced him to relinquish his inheritance.

Lady Foresight

But that will not prevent Angelica from marrying him. She is a romantic fool, but she has ample fortune in her own hands.

Maskwell

You have already been tampering with Lady Froth?

Lady Foresight

I have. She is ready for any impression I think fit.

Maskwell

She must be thoroughly persuaded that Valentine loves her.

Lady Foresight

She is so credulous and she likes him—likes any man—so well that she will believe it faster than I can persuade her. She will write an epic about it. But, what can we gain that way?

Maskwell

Time. Come, we must speak of this privately.

(Exit Maskwell and Lady Foresight.)

ACT I
SCENE 2

The same, later that day.

Enter Foresight and Lady Foresight.

Foresight

I confess I am troubled that you are so cold in his defense.

Lady Foresight

His defense! Bless me, would you have me defend an ill thing?

Foresight

You believe Lady Froth then?

Lady Foresight

I don't know. I find you are prepared to receive an ill impression of any opinion of mine that is not agreeable to your own. But, as I am like to be censured in the end, I do not believe it. Don't ask me my reasons, they are not fit to be told.

Foresight

Reasons that convince you, ought to convince me.

Lady Foresight

If I told you I saw it in the stars or in a dream, you would believe me.

Foresight

Did you?

Lady Foresight

I have better proof than that. (cagily) Don't press me.

Foresight

This Valentine, although he has forfeited his fortune, I have always regarded as a decent man, suitable for Angelica, if she would have him. But, I will not allow her to marry a libertine. Now, speak.

Lady Foresight

What ever it was, it's past. Rest satisfied.

Foresight

When you have told me, I will.

Lady Foresight

You won't.

Foresight

I will.

Lady Foresight

What if you can't?

Foresight

Then I must know. No more trifling.

Lady Foresight

Don't be in a passion. You shan't be angry.

Foresight

Well, well.

Lady Foresight

You will be calm. Indeed, it's nothing—but— (a pregnant pause)

Foresight

But what?

Lady Foresight

But, you must promise not to be angry. Valentine is very sorry. He swore he was sorry—and would not do it again.

Foresight

Sorry for what?

Lady Foresight

No great matter, only—well, I have your promise. Only Valentine had a mind to amuse himself with a little gallantry toward me.

Foresight (angry)

What?

Mrs. Foresight

I can't think he meant it seriously.

Foresight

By all the signs in the Zodiac!

Lady Foresight

Or maybe he thought he was not close enough kin to me—and had a mind to create a nearer relation of his own—a lover, you know. Well, but that's all. You see it was nothing. Now you have it. Nothing to take notice about.

Foresight

May the powers of hell smite him.

Lady Foresight

A little harmless mirth—only misplaced, that's all. It's over now. What if his hand did—

Foresight

Did—did what?

Lady Foresight

I'm sure he didn't mean to touch my breast. For my part, I have forgot it; I hope he can. I'm sure he has, for I have not heard from him for these two days.

Foresight

Two days! Is it so fresh? I'll have him beaten.

Lady Foresight

Oh, for heaven's sake. You'll ruin me if you take such public notice of it.

Foresight

Before I've done, I will be satisfied. How long?

Lady Foresight

How long what?

Foresight

How long did he touch it?

Lady Foresight

Lord, I don't know. A minute, perhaps, before I freed myself.

Foresight

By all the stars in the firmament, I am provoked into a fermentation.

Lady Foresight

Have patience, let me alone to rattle him up.

Foresight

Give me leave to be angry. I'll rattle him up. I'll firk him with a certiorari.

Lady Foresight

You firk him—I'll firk him myself, be content.

Foresight

Content yourself! Passion is coming upon me by inflation. I cannot submit as formerly, therefore, give way.

Lady Foresight

What! Will you be pleased to retire and—

Foresight

No, I will not be pleased to retire. I am pleased to be angry, that's my pleasure at this time.

Lady Foresight

Why, who are you? What am I? Can't I govern you? What did I marry you for? Am I not absolute and uncontrollable? Is it fit that a woman of my spirit and conduct should be contradicted in a matter of this concern?

Foresight

It concerns me and only me. Besides, I am not to be governed at all times. When I am in tranquility, my lady shall command, but when I am provoked to fury, I cannot incorporate with patience and reason. I tell you Mars is in the ascendant; I am ready, I am ready! (brandishing his cane about like a weapon)

Lady Foresight

Hot-headed still! Remember, I have a bedtime lecture for you, you disobedient, headstrong brute.

Foresight

It's because I won't be a brute with horns that I am thus exasperated. I will protect my honor.

Lady Foresight

Your honor! You have none but what is in my keeping, and I can dispose of it when I please—therefore don't provoke me.

(Angelica and Valentine approach.)

Lady Foresight (to Valentine)

Inhuman and treacherous—

Foresight (finishing her sentence)

—serpent.

Angelica

Bless me!

Foresight

Niece, Niece, come away. Go not near him; there's nothing but deceit in him.

Lady Foresight

Impudent creature!

Valentine

For heaven's sake, madame, to whom do you direct this language?

Lady Foresight

Have I behaved myself with all the decorum and nicety befitting the wife of a great astrologer? Have I preserved my honor, white and unsullied, for all these years—and lately even from my husband—to be thus insulted?

Foresight

She's been an invincible wife, even to me—

Lady Foresight

Have I, I say, preserved myself like a fair sheet of paper for you to make a blot upon?

Foresight

And she shall make a simile with any woman in England? Do you think that my niece is fit for nothing but a stalking horse while you take aim at my wife?

Lady Foresight

Take the child from his sight.

Angelica

He's innocent. I'm sure.

Foresight

Innocent! He cares nothing for you but for your fortune, and he's in love with my wife. If I should ever have horns, they will kill me; they would never come kindly. I should die of them like a child cutting his teeth. Come, come.

(Foresight forcibly drags the protesting Angelica away.)

Valentine

I still don't understand.

Lady Foresight

You cannot dare deny it.

Valentine

I still don't know—

Lady Foresight

Fiddle, faddle, don't tell me of this and that. How could you think to make the—the daughter the means of procuring the mother?

Valentine

The daughter to procure the mother!

Lady Foresight

Though I'm not Angelica's real mother, I've practically been one to her—and that's near enough to make it incest.

Valentine

Incest!

Lady Foresight

Reflect on the horror of it. Consider what you would have to answer for, should you provoke me to weakness. I, I who have trod the road of virtue thus long and never made one trip, not one false step!

Valentine

Where am I? Is it day? Am I awake?

Lady Foresight

And nobody knows what may happen. I am sure I can resist the strongest temptation, but then there's no certainty in this life.

Valentine

Madame, pray give me leave to ask you one question.

Lady Foresight

Ask me the question. I swear I'll refuse it! Oh, you have brought all the blood into my face.

Valentine

Madame, hear me—

Lady Foresight

Hear you? No, no—I'll deny you first and hear you afterward.

Valentine

For heaven's sake, madame.

Lady Foresight

Bless me, how can you talk of heaven? Name it no more. Maybe you don't think it a sin, maybe it is not sin to them that don't think so. If I did not think it a sin, I—

Valentine (dropping to his knees)

Madame, on my knees—

Lady Foresight

No, no, rise up. I know love is powerful, and nobody can help his passion. It's not your fault. I swear it is a pity it should be a fault, but my honor, well, but your honor, too—but the sin—well, but—oh, Lord, someone's coming. I dare not stay. Strive against it, but don't be melancholy. But never think of marrying Angelica, for though I know you don't love her, yet it will make me jealous. I must fly.

(Lady Foresight exits. Maskwell enters by another

door.)

Valentine (rising)

Maskwell, welcome. The witch has raised the storm and her ministers have done their work; you see the vessels are parted.

Maskwell

I know it. I met Foresight towing away Angelica. Come, don't trouble yourself. I'll join you together or drown in the attempt.

Valentine

There's comfort in a hand stretched out to a drowning man.

Maskwell

Not drowning. Come, cheer up. Lady Foresight has given me a retaining fee. I am your greatest enemy and she does but journeyman's work under my supervision.

Valentine

How's this?

Maskwell

What do you think of my being employed in the execution of her plots? By heaven, it's true. I have undertaken to break the match and make your father disinherit you. Oh, she has opened her heart to me. I am to turn you grazing and marry Angelica myself.

Valentine

How I shall praise you. You have outwitted Woman.

Maskwell

She was very violent at first.

Valentine

A very fury; but I am afraid of her violence at last.

Maskwell

I know her temper. I pretended to be secretly in love with Angelica; that did my business and convinced Lady Foresight that I might be trusted.

Valentine

I am lucky in having you for a friend.

Maskwell

Though I say it myself, I am resourceful.

CURTAIN

ACT I
SCENE 3

A MIMED INTERLUDE.

Foresight and Mrs. Foresight vociferate with Angelica denouncing Valentine. Valentine succeeds in presenting his case to Angelica and convinces her that Mrs. Foresight was mistaken as to his intentions, and that he was only addressing her in the hopes of softening her so he could marry Angelica.

Now, when Foresight and Mrs. Foresight renew the attack on Valentine, Angelica forcefully defends Valentine. Afraid that Angelica will marry Valentine despite her family's opposition, and fearing her game is backfiring Mrs. Foresight consults Maskwell.

Maskwell, suggests that Angelica be conciliated, so that she will revert to her usual maddening behavior; Mrs. Foresight and Maskwell convince Foresight to set a trap for Valentine. Foresight is difficult to convince but is finally persuaded by an omen. Foresight apologizes to Valentine although he is still suspicious that Valentine hankers after his wife.

Angelica, no longer obliged to defend Valentine, is a bit suspicious and begins to revert to her capricious ways. Stunned, Valentine is ready to pull out his hair.

SHORT CURTAIN

ACT II
SCENE 4

Same as Act I, later that day.

Enter Mrs. Frail, in a fury. She is followed by Lady Foresight.

Mrs. Frail

What have you to do to watch me? S'life, I'll do what I please.

Lady Foresight

You will?

Mrs. Frail

Yes, a great piece of business about taking a turn in a coach with a friend.

Lady Foresight

Two or three turns, I'll take my oath.

Mrs. Frail

Well, what if I took twenty? Surely if you had done it, it had only been innocent recreation. Lord, where's the comfort in this life, if we can't have the happiness of conversing with whom we like?

Lady Foresight

But, can't you converse at home? I own it, I think there's no happiness like conversing with an agreeable man; I don't quarrel at that, and I'm sure your conversation was very innocent; but the place is public, and to be seen in a coach with a man is scandalous. What if anybody else had seen you as I did? It would not only reflect on you, Sister, but on me.

Mrs. Frail

Pooh! Why should it reflect upon you? I don't doubt but you have made yourself happy in a coach before now—

Lady Foresight

You forget yourself! I am your brother's wife!

Mrs. Frail

If I had gone to Chelsea or Knightsbridge with a man, something might have been said—

Lady Foresight

Why, was I ever in one of those places? What do you mean, Sister?

Mrs. Frail

Mean? Nothing, not I.

Lady Foresight (furious)

You have been at a worse place.

Mrs. Frail

I, at a worse place? And with a man?

Lady Foresight

I suppose you are not shameless enough to go alone to Black Peter's?

Mrs. Frail

Black Peter's? What's that?

Lady Foresight

Poor innocent! You don't know that there's a place called Black Peter's! You'd make an admirable actress, you can keep your face straight enough.

Mrs. Frail

I'll swear you've got a great deal of confidence and, to my mind, too much for the stage.

Lady Foresight

Very well, that will appear. You were never at Black Peter's?

Mrs. Frail

No.

Lady Foresight

You deny it, positively, to my face?

Mrs. Frail

Your face? What's your face?

Lady Foresight

No matter for that—it's as good as yours.

Mrs. Frail

But slightly more shopworn. But I do deny it, positively, to your face. There!

Lady Foresight

Do you so? But look here now. Where did you lose this garter? Oh, Sister, Sister.

Mrs. Frail

My garter!

Lady Foresight

It's yours. Look at it.

Mrs. Frail

Well, if it goes to that—where did you find it? Oh, Sister, Sister. Sister, every way.

Lady Foresight (helplessly)

Er—someone found it and gave it to me on your account.

Mrs. Frail

Pshaw! That won't pass. I have heard it said that in fencing one should take care not to expose oneself when making a thrust.

Lady Foresight

Very true. We are both wounded—so let us do what

duelists often do— take care of one another and grow better friends than before.

Mrs. Frail

With all my heart. Ours are but slight wounds, and if we keep them well covered, not in the least dangerous.

Lady Foresight

Shh! Someone's coming.

(Enter Lady Froth and Tattle at another door.)

Lady Froth

Then, you think that the episode between Susan, the dairy maid, and the coachman is not amiss.

Tattle

Incomparable, let me perish—but then, being an heroic poem, had you not better call him a charioteer?

Lady Froth

Oh, infinitely better; I'm extremely beholden to you for the hint. (declaiming) "For as the Sun shines every day, So of our coach man I may say—"

Tattle

Incomparable, egad—but I have one exception to make. Don't you think there should be marginal notes to the whole poem?

Lady Froth

I like that thought. You'd oblige me extremely to write notes to the whole poem—

Tattle

With all my heart and soul and, proud of the vast honor, let me perish.

Lady Froth

Ah, there's my dear Mrs. Frail; servant Lady Foresight.

(Enter Lord Froth.)

Lord Froth

My dear, have you done? We were just laughing at my Lady Wishfort and Mr. Sneer.

Lady Froth

Oh, filthy Mr. Sneer—he spent two days trying to match the color of his coach with his complexion.

Lord Froth

Yet his Aunt is as fond of him as if she whelped him herself.

Lady Foresight

My Lady Toothless. She's a mortifying spectacle; she's always chewing cud like an old ewe.

Mrs. Frail

Then, there's that other great strapping friend of hers—Lady—I can't think of her name—the one that paints so exorbitantly.

Tattle

Paints, d'ye say. Why, she lays it on with a trowel—let me perish.

Lord Froth

I made a song of her.

Lady Froth

Oh, let's hear it.

Lord Froth

Ancient Phyllis has young graces, 'Tis a strange thing,

but a true one. Shall I tell you how? She herself makes her own faces, And each morning wears a new one. Where's the wonder now?

(Everyone laughs and applauds, most notably, Lady Froth, who admires extravagantly everything her husband does.)

Lady Froth

Very pretty. My Lord, I have been telling Mrs. Frail how much I have been in love with you. Ha, ha, ha. Do you remember, my Lord? (squeezing him and giving him a fond look, sighing and then laughing)

Lord Froth

Pleasant creature! Perfectly well. Who could resist?

Lady Froth

Oh, that tongue, that dear deceitful tongue. Was ever anything so well bred as my Lord?

Tattle

Never anything but your ladyship, let me perish.

Lady Froth

Doesn't Mr. Tattle have a deal of wit?

Lord Froth

Oh, yes, madame.

Tattle (protesting)

Oh, heavens, madame.

Lady Froth

More wit than anybody.

Tattle

I'm everlastingly your humble servant.

Lord Froth

Don't you think us a happy couple?

Mrs. Frail

I think you the happiest couple in the world, for you're not only happy in one another when you are together, but happy in yourselves and by yourselves.

Lady Froth (to Lady Foresight)

I am sure Cousin Foresight makes you a good husband—

Lady Foresight

Foh—

Tattle

My Lord was telling me that Your Ladyship was composing an epic poem.

Lady Froth

Did my Lord tell you? It's true, and the subject is my Lord's love to me. What do you think I call it? You won't guess. Spumoso.

Mrs. Frail

Spumoso?

Lady Froth

Italian for Froth.

Lady Foresight

Very apropos, ha, ha, ha.

Lady Froth (to Tattle)

You must be my confidant. Ha, ha, ha.

(Enter Miss Prue, a pretty, well-developed girl of fifteen, but dressed as a child with pigtails and bows, etc.)

Prue (excited)

Mother, Mother, Mother, look you here!

Lady Foresight

Fie, fie, Miss Prue, how you bawl. Besides, I have told you, you must not call me Mother.

Prue (puzzled)

What must I call you then, Mama?

Lady Foresight

Laetitia. You must say Laetitia. As I am a person, I shall be fancied old indeed to have this great girl call me Mother. Well, but what are you so overjoyed at?

Prue

Look you here, Laetitia, then—what Lord Froth has given me. Here's a snuff box—how sweet it is. Lord Froth is all over sweet. His wig is sweet; his gloves are sweet; and his breath is pure sweet. He gave me this ring for a kiss—

Lord Froth (not in the least embarrassed)

Oh, fie, Miss, you must not kiss and tell.

Prue

Yes, I may tell my Mother—I mean Laetitia. And he says he'll give me something to make my smock smell sweet.

Lady Foresight

Oh, fie, Miss, amongst your linen. You must never say smock.

Prue

Why, it's not bawdy, is it?

Lord Froth

You are too severe upon Miss. Her simplicity becomes her strangely. Don't let them persuade you out of your innocence.

Lady Foresight

I wish you don't persuade her out of her innocence. You damn toad.

Lord Froth

Who, I, madame? How can you have such a thought? You don't know me. I adore my wife and am as chaste as she.

Lady Foresight (aside)

Then she's lost.

Lady Froth

I trust my Lord as I do myself. A little innocent raillery.

Lord Froth

I swear I would not for the world—

Lady Foresight

Oh, hang you; who'd believe you? I know you, sir—

Lord Froth

How you love to jest, Cousin.

Lady Froth

Why did you have to see her before she was married. Now she'll never marry that uncouth sailor my husband proposes for her.

Lord Froth

Upon reputation—

Lady Foresight

If my husband found me with you, he'd swear I deliberately brought you acquainted.

Lord Froth

I assure you, madame—

Lady Foresight

But, then leaving you together, is just as bad. You're too sly a devil to miss such an opportunity. Well, I don't care. I won't have seen it. I wash my hands of it, I'm thoroughly innocent. You will have a lot to answer for if you do. Ladies, come to cards. (to Lady Froth) Aren't you afraid to leave your husband with such an innocent girl?

Lady Froth

Not I. I trust him as I do myself.

Tattle

I shall follow Your Ladyship.

(Lady Foresight, Mrs. Frail, Lady Froth and Tattle exit.)

Prue

What makes Mother go away, my Lord? What does

she mean, do you know?

Lord Froth

Yes, my dear, I think I can guess. But I'm damned if I've ever seen the like.

Prue

Come, must we not go, too?

Lord Froth (hesitating, then deciding)

No, no. She doesn't mean that.

Prue

No! What then? What shall you and I do together?

Lord Froth

I must make love to you, pretty miss: will you let me?

Prue

Yes, if you please.

Lord Froth (aside)

Frank at least. What kind of mother is this? Is it to make a fool of me, or does she do as she would be done by? I'll understand it that way.

Prue

Come, I long to have you begin. Must I make love, too? You must tell me how.

Lord Froth

You must let me speak, Miss. You must not speak first; I must ask you questions and you must answer.

Prue

What, is it like the catechism? Come then, ask me.

Lord Froth

Do you think you can love me?

Prue

Yes.

Lord Froth

Pooh, you must not say "yes" already. I shan't care a damn for you if you answer so readily.

Prue (puzzled)

What must I say, then?

Lord Froth

You must say "no" or "I believe not" or "I can't tell."

Prue

What, must I tell you a lie, then?

Lord Froth

Yes, if you would be well bred. Besides, you are a woman and must never speak what you think. Your words must contradict your thoughts, but your actions may contradict your words. So, when I ask you if you love me, you must say no, but you must love me—or at least make me think you do. If I tell you that you are handsome, you must deny it and scorn flattery, yet think yourself more becoming than any other woman. If I ask you to kiss me, you must be angry, but you must not refuse me. If I ask you for more, you must be more angry, but more complying, and as soon as I make you say you'll scream if I don't stop—you must be sure to hold your tongue—

Prue

Oh, I like this rarely. And must you not lie, too?

Lord Froth

Hum—yes. But you must believe I speak the truth.

Prue

Oh, Gemini! Well, I always had a great mind to tell lies, but they frightened me and said it was a sin.

Lord Froth

Well, my pretty creature, will you make me happy by giving me a kiss?

Prue

No, indeed; I'm angry with you for asking.

(Prue throws her arms around Lord Froth's neck and kisses him.)

Lord Froth

Hold, hold, that's pretty well. But, you shouldn't have given it to me, but rather, permitted me to steal it.

Prue

Well, let's try again.

Lord Froth

With all my heart. Now then, my little angel. (kissing her)

Prue

Pish.

Lord Froth

That's right, again, my charmer.

Prue

Now, I can't abide you.

Lord Froth

Admirable! You might have been born and bred in London. And won't you show me your bed chamber?

Prue

No, indeed. But, I'll run there and hide under the bedcover.

Lord Froth

I'll follow you.

Prue

Ah, but I'll hold the door with both hands and be angry; and you shall push me down before you come in.

Lord Froth

No, I'll come in first, and push you down afterwards.

Prue

Will you? Then, I'll be more angry and more willing.

Lord Froth

Then, I'll make you scream.

Prue

Oh, but you shan't, for I'll hold my tongue.

Lord Froth

Oh, my apt scholar.

Prue

Now, I'll run away.

Lord Froth

Now, I'll follow.

(Exit Prue, followed with Lord Froth. Enter Tattle.)

Tattle (musing)

Ah, my dear Lady Froth. She's a most engaging creature, nearly as affected as I am—if only she were not so fond of that damned coxcombly Lord of hers. Now, what shall I say to her? Pox on it—none but dull rogues think—witty men like rich fellows are ready for all expenses. Here she comes. (walks about, singing) I'm sick with love, Prithee come cure me—

(Enter Lady Froth.)

Lady Froth

Have you seen my Lord?

Tattle

Oh, my dear Lady Froth! 'Gad, I thank you.

Lady Froth

Oh, heavens, Mr. Tattle! What's the matter?

Tattle

The matter, madame? Why, nothing—nothing at all!

Lady Froth

Why did you call out upon me so loud?

Tattle

When?

Lady Froth

Just now. Why, don't you know it?

Tattle

Did I! Strange. See how love and murder will out.

Lady Froth

Do you talk of love? Oh, Parnassus, who would have thought Mr. Tattle could be in love? I thought you could have no mistress but the nine muses.

Tattle

No more have I. I adore them all in Your Ladyship. Deuce take me if I can tell whether I am happy or sad that Your Ladyship has made this discovery.

Lady Froth

Oh, be merry, by all means. Ha, ha, ha.

Tattle

Oh, barbarous, to turn me to ridicule! Yet, ha, ha, ha. Deuce take me, I can't help laughing myself. Ha, ha, ha; yet, by heavens, I have a violent passion for Your Ladyship.

Lady Froth

Seriously, ha, ha, ha?

Tattle

Seriously, ha, ha, ha.

Lady Froth

What—ha, ha, ha d'ye think I laugh at? Ha, ha, ha.

Tattle

Me, ha, ha, ha.

Lady Froth

No, the deuce take me if I don't laugh at myself, for hang me if I have not a violent passion for Mr. Tattle, ha, ha, ha.

Tattle

Seriously?

Lady Froth

Seriously, ha, ha, ha.

Tattle

Let me perish, ha, ha, ha. Ah, my dear charming Lady Froth.

Lady Froth

Oh, my adored Mr. Tattle.

(They embrace. While Lady Froth and Tattle embrace, enter Lord Froth and Miss Prue, hurriedly. The couples do not see each other. Lord Froth is hurriedly dressing, Prue is struggling with her clothes. Lady Froth and Tattle continue to embrace.)

Lord Froth

Pox take your old Nurse. Never was man so unkindly interrupted.

(Lord Froth puts on his wig.)

Miss Prue

She'll tell my father. What shall I do? What lie can I tell?

Lord Froth

There's no occasion for a lie. I never could tell a lie to no purpose. Why, we have done nothing, have we, child? Therefore, say nothing, but deny everything. It's best I leave you. Come off as best you can.

(Lord Froth pushes Prue back the way she came, straightens his wig, and advances in the direction of Tattle and Lady Froth.)

Tattle

Zoons, madame, there's my Lord.

Lady Froth

Take no notice. Now, cast off and meet me at the lower end of the room. Oh, here's my Lord, now you shall see me do it with him. (to Lord Froth) Shall you and I do our close dance to show Mr. Tattle? (not noticing her husband closely)

Lord Froth (eager to escape)

No, my dear, do it with him.

Lady Froth

I'll do it with him when you are out of the way.

Tattle

That's good. I can hardly hold laughing.

Lord Froth

Any other time, my dear.

(Exit Lord Froth, not paying attention to his wife.)

Lady Froth

Shall we do it?

Tattle

With all my heart.

CURTAIN

ACT III
SCENE 5

Same as Act I, the next morning.

Servant

Sir, my Lady is dressing.

Ben

Dressing! Then, my Aunt hasn't dined yet?

Servant

Your Aunt, sir?

Ben

My Aunt, yes, my Aunt, and Your Lady! How long have you lived with the lady, eh?

Servant

A week, sir. Longer than anybody else.

Ben

No doubt you know her if you see her.

Servant

I cannot safely swear to her face in the morning.

Ben

Well, try what you can. Search and tell her that Ben Plyant is in the house.

Servant

Yes, sir. Will you step this way, sir?

Ben

This creature knows less than a starling; I doubt it knows it's own name.

(Exit Ben, following the Servant. Enter at another door: Angelica and Mrs. Foresight.)

Angelica (in a pet)

Sure, never anything was so unbred as that odious man!

Lady Foresight

You have a color, what's the matter?

Angelica

That horrid fellow Petulant has provoked me into a flame. I have broken my fan. Is not all the powder out of my hair?

Lady Foresight

No. What has he done?

Angelica

He has done nothing; he has only contradicted everything that I said. Well, it is a lamentable thing, I swear, that one has not the liberty of choosing one's acquaintances as one does one's clothes.

Lady Foresight

Fools never wear out. If one could only give them to one's maid after a day or two.

Angelica

Better so, indeed.

Lady Foresight

If you would but admit Valentine as your gallant, you might easily discard Witwould and Petulant as your old smock. And, indeed, it is time, for the town has found it.

Angelica

The town has found it! What has the town found? That Valentine loves me is no secret.

Lady Foresight

You are nettled.

Angelica

You're mistaken. Ridiculous!

Lady Foresight

Indeed, my dear, you'll tear another fan if you don't mitigate those violent airs.

Angelica

Oh, silly! Ha, ha, ha. I could laugh immoderately. Poor Valentine. I swear I never commanded him to be so coy. If I had the vanity to think he would obey me, I would command him to show you more gallantry. But I despair to prevail, and so, let him have his own way.

Ha, ha, ha. Pardon me, dear creature, I must laugh. Ha, ha, ha, though I grant you, it is a little barbarous, ha, ha, ha.

Lady Foresight

What a pity it is so much fine raillery and delivered with so significant gesture should be unhappily directed to miscarry.

Angelica

Ha? Dear creature, I ask your pardon. I swear I did not mind you.

Lady Foresight

Shall I tell him by telling you—?

Angelica

Oh dear, what? For it is the same thing if I hear it. Ha, ha, ha.

Lady Foresight

That I detest him, hate him, madame—

Angelica

Oh, madame, so do I. And yet the creature loves me, ha, ha, ha. How can one not laugh to think of it? I'll take my death I can't think what he sees in me. I'll swear you are handsomer, and within a year or two as young—and so much more experienced. If you could but stay for me, I should overtake you. Well, that thought makes me melancholic, now I'll be sad—

Lady Foresight

You are merry, Angelica. (aside) Your merry note may be changed sooner than you think. (aloud) From your example I learn that if we will be happy, we must find the means in ourselves, not in men. Men are always in extremes—while they dote, their jealousies are insupportable; and when they cease to love, they loathe.

Angelica

It's an unhappy circumstance that the man should so often outlive the lover. But, 'tis better to be deserted than never to have loved. For my part, my youth may waste, but it shall never rust.

Lady Foresight

Then it seems you dissemble an aversion to men?

Angelica

Certainly. To have greater freedom.

Lady Foresight

Are you a libertine?

Angelica

Be sincere. Acknowledge that your sentiments agree with mine.

Lady Foresight

Never.

Angelica

You hate men?

Lady Foresight

Heartily, inveterately.

Angelica

Your husband?

Lady Foresight

Most transcendentally, and though I say it, meritoriously.

Angelica

Give me your hand upon it.

Lady Foresight

There.

Angelica

I join with you. What I said was but to test you.

Lady Foresight

Is it possible? Do you hate those vipers, men?

Angelica

I have done hating them and am now come to despise them; the next thing I have to do is eternally to forget them.

Lady Foresight

There spoke the spirit of an amazon.

Angelica

And yet, I am thinking to carry my aversion further.

Lady Foresight

How?

Angelica

By marrying. If I could find one thoroughly sensible

of ill usage, I think I should revenge myself that way.

Lady Foresight

Would you make him a cuckold?

Angelica

At the very least, I would make him think I would.

Lady Foresight

Why not do it?

Angelica

Well, I might. But if he should ever discover it, he would know the worst and be out of his pain.

Lady Foresight

Ingenious mischief. Would you were married to Valentine.

Angelica

Would I were.

Lady Foresight

You change color.

Angelica

Because I hate him.

Lady Foresight

Why so do I, but I can hear him named.

Angelica

I think you look a little pale.

Lady Foresight

Do I? I think I am a little sick on the sudden.

Angelica

What ails you?

Lady Foresight

My husband. Don't you see him? He's in the next room with Valentine.

Angelica

Ha, ha, ha. He comes opportunely for you.

Lady Foresight

For you he has brought Valentine.

Foresight (coming forward)

My dear.

Lady Foresight

My soul.

Foresight

You don't look well today, child.

Lady Foresight

Do you think so?

Angelica

He is the only man that does, madame.

Lady Foresight

The only man that would tell me so, at least. And the only man from whom I can hear it without mortification.

(to Angelica) I shall leave you to your lover, for I know you are dying to see him. Don't deny it. But, your tune will soon change.

Angelica

Do you say so? Then, I'm resolved to enjoy it while it lasts. (declaiming) I alone that conquest prize When I insult a rival's eyes— If there's delight in love, 'tis when I see, That heart which others bleed for, Bleed for me.

Lady Foresight

Come, Foresight, we must go.

Foresight

Mr. Valentine has waited this half hour for an opportunity to talk with you. Shall I tell him you are at leisure?

Angelica

No. What would the dear man have? Bid him come another day. Or send him hither. Just as you will. I think I'll see him, shall I? Yes, let the wretch come. (to Lady Foresight) Entertain Valentine, Aunt. You have the philosophy to undergo a fool—you are married and have learned patience.

Lady Foresight

I am obliged to you for making me your proxy in this affair, but I have business of my own.

(Exit Lady Foresight and Foresight.)

Valentine (coming forward)

Do you lock yourself up from me to make my search more difficult? Or does it signify that the chase must end, for you can fly no more?

Angelica

Vanity! No. I'll fly and be followed till the last moment. To the very last, and afterwards.

Valentine

What after the last?

Angelica

I should think I was poor indeed if I were freed from the agreeable fatigues of solicitation. I hate a lover that dares to think he can draw a moment's breath but for my unparalleled bounty. There is not so impudent a thing in nature as the saucy look of an assured man confident of success. Ah, I'll never marry unless I am first made sure of my will and pleasure.

Valentine

Would you have them both now before marriage, or will you be content with the first now and stay for the other until after grace?

Angelica

Don't be impudent. Dear liberty, shall I give thee up? I can't do it. It is more than impossible. Positively, Valentine, I'll lie abed in a morning as long as I please.

Valentine

Then I'll get up as early as I please.

Angelica

Get up when you will, idle creature. D'ye hear, I won't be called names after I'm married. Positively, I won't be called names.

Valentine

Names!

Angelica

Yes, such as wife, spouse, dear, joy, jewel, love, sweetheart and the rest of that nauseous cant! I shall never bear that. Good Valentine, don't let us be fond. Let us never visit together—nor go to a play together—let us be very distant and well bred. Let us be as well bred as if we had been married a great while, and as coy as if we were not married at all.

Valentine

Have you any conditions to offer. Thus far your demands are pretty reasonable.

Angelica

Trifles. Liberty to pay and receive visits to and from whom I please without interrogations or wry faces on your part; to wear what I please, to converse with no man friend of yours that I don't like, come to dinner when I like or not, if I don't like, and not to be obligated to give a reason. And lastly where ever I am, you shall always knock at the door before you come in. And no peeping. I will not be peeped at. These articles subscribed to, if I continue to endure you a little longer, I may, by degrees, dwindle into a wife.

Valentine

All I ask is that when you dwindle into a wife, I am not enlarged into a husband.

Angelica

Propose your utmost; speak and spare not.

Valentine

I thank you. First, you must admit no sworn confidant or intimate of your own sex; no she-friend to screen her affairs under your countenance, and tempt you to do the like. No decoy duck to wheedle you a fop or to go to the play in a mask.

Angelica

Detestable condition! I go to the play in a mask?

Valentine

Item I, Article: that you continue to like your own face as long as I shall, and that while it passes current with me, that you not endeavor to new coin it. To which end I prohibit all masks for the night made of oilskins, puppy water and I know not what. Item: when you shall be breeding—

Angelica

Oh, name it not.

Valentine

Which may be presumed as a blessing on our endeavors—

Angelica

Odious endeavor!

Valentine

There will be no straight lacing and squeezing till you

mold my boy's head like a sausage loaf. These provisos admitted in other things I may prove a tractable and good-natured husband.

Angelica

Oh, horrid proviso. I hate your proviso.

Valentine

Shall I kiss your hand upon the contract?

Angelica

What must I do? Shall I have him? I think I must have him. Well then, I'll take my death, I'm in a horrid fright. I shall never say it. Well, I think I'll endure you.

Valentine

Speak in plain terms. Tell me, for I am sure you have a mind to me.

Angelica

Are you? I think I have—and you, horrid man, you look as if you thought so, too. Well, you ridiculous thing you, I'll have you— I won't be kissed, and I won't be thanked. Here, kiss my hand, though. (Valentine kisses her hand) So, hold your tongue now, don't say a word.

Valentine

I am all obedience. But I shall release you from your promise if I am not able to regain my inheritance.

Angelica

Never mind that. My fortune is large enough for two.

Valentine

I must have it, or I will never marry you.

Angelica

If you talk like this we shall quarrel.

Valentine

A man has his honor.

Angelica

Damn your honor. I will marry you immediately or not at all.

Valentine

We must wait. I have a plan.

Angelica

Never mind your plans. I will have you now.

Valentine

Be patient.

Angelica

No. If I must be patient, I take it back.

Valentine

But, Angelica—

Angelica

No.

Valentine (furious)

Be it so.

(Valentine stalks off.)

Angelica

Foolish man. I will never marry him.

(Enter Sir Sampson, Prue, and Mrs. Frail.)

Sir Sampson

What, is Valentine sneaked off and would not wait to see his brother? There's an unnatural whelp—there's an unnatural dog. What, you here, too, madame, and could not keep him? Madame, he is not worth your consideration.

Angelica (controlling herself and engaging in duplicity)

I'm pretty even with him, Sir Sampson, for if ever I could have liked anything about him, it would have been his money, but since that's gone, the bait's off and the naked hook appears.

Sir Sampson

Well said; you are a wiser woman than I thought you; most young women nowadays are to be tempted with a naked hook.

Angelica (coyly)

I'm for money with any man or for any man with money. I declare I had rather have you than your son.

Sir Sampson

Is that so? I'm glad to hear you say so. I was afraid you were in love with the reprobate and would marry him without a penny.

Angelica

Never! (suppressing tears)

Sir Sampson (to himself)

Wouldn't that be revenge, hey? Marry her myself. I'll think on it.

(Enter Ben.)

Ben

Where's Father?

Sampson

Son, Ben! Bless the dear boy. You are heartily welcome.

Ben

Thank you, Father. I'm glad to see you again.

Sir Sampson

Kiss me, dear boy.

Ben (freeing himself)

Enough, Father, I'd rather kiss these gentlewomen.

Sir Sampson

And so you shall. Angelica, my son, Ben.

Ben (kissing Angelica)

If you please. Nay, ma'am, I'm not dropping anchor here. (kissing Frail) About ship, and you too, little cock boat.

Prue

Foh.

Angelica

Welcome ashore.

Ben

Thank you. Well, Father, how do all at home? How does Brother Dick and Brother Val?

Sir Sampson

Dick? Dick has been dead these two years. I wrote you when you were at Gibraltar.

Ben

That's true, I had forgotten. No wonder he didn't write. I have many questions to ask you.

Sir Sampson

I intend you shall marry, Ben.

Ben

I have no mind to marry. It's a dangerous voyage, d'ye see.

Mrs. Frail

That would be a pity, such a handsome young gentleman. (aside) And like to be so rich. Why should that little chit (indicating Prue) have him?

Ben

Handsome! (laughing) If you be for joking, I'll joke with you.

Sir Sampson

Ben's a wag.

Ben

A man that is married is chained to an oar all his life, and mayhap forced to tug a leaky vessel into the bargain.

Sir Sampson (a little embarrassed)

Ben's a wag—only he wants a little polishing.

Mrs. Frail

Say you so? Not at all, I like his humor. I should like such humor in a husband extremely—

Ben

And I should like such a handsome wench for a bedfellow; how say you, mistress, would you like to be going to sea? You're a tight vessel and well rigged—were you but as well manned.

Angelica

I swear Mr. Benjamin is an absolute sea-wit.

Sir Sampson (growing more uncomfortable)

Ben has parts, but as I said before, they want a little polishing: you must not take anything ill, madame.

Mrs. Frail

I'm not offended. But you should leave him alone with his mistress. (whispering to Ben) I should not doubt that I would be well manned if you were master of me.

Sir Sampson

You're right. Look you, Ben, this lady (presenting Prue) is to be your wife. Come, Miss, you must not be shamefaced. We'll leave you together.

Prue

I can't abide to be left alone. May my cousin stay with me?

Sir Sampson

No, no. Let's leave them.

Ben

Father, perhaps the young woman mayn't take a liking to me.

Sir Sampson

Don't worry. Come, we'll be gone.

(Enter Foresight as Sir Sampson, Mrs. Frail and Angelica are leaving.)

Foresight

What, is he come? Are they together?

Sir Sampson

Yes, yes. What if he should not stop to say grace, old Foresight; but fall to without the help of a parson, ha? Odd, I could not be angry with him. It would but be like me. Ha, thou art melancholic old prognosticator. Come, come, cheer up, Old Stargazer.

Foresight (serious)

We'll have the wedding tomorrow morning.

Sir Sampson

With all my heart.

Foresight

At ten o'clock, punctually at ten.

Sir Sampson

To a minute, to a second. They shall be married to a minute, go to bed a minute, and—

Mrs. Frail

Manners!

(They go out, Sir Sampson apologizing.)

Ben

Come, Miss, will you please to sit down? I'll hand you a chair.

(Prue shakes her head.)

Ben

If you stand astern like that, we shall never grapple

together.

(Prue reluctantly sits.)

Ben

There. I'll sit near you.

Prue (moving her chair back as he moves forward)

I can hear you farther off; I ain't deaf.

Ben

I'll heave off to please you. (moves farther off) Look you, Miss, I am bound for the land of matrimony, a voyage that was none of my seeking, and mayhap, I may steer into your harbor.

Prue

Don't talk bawdy to me!

Ben

The short of the thing is, that if you like me, and I like you, we may chance to swing in a hammock together.

Prue

I don't know what to say to you, and I don't care to speak to you at all.

Ben

No? I'm sorry for that. But, why are you so scornful?

Prue

As long as one must not speak one's mind, one had best not speak at all, I think, and truly, I won't tell a lie, for that matter.

Ben

True. That's to look one way and now another. I'm not for keeping anything under hatches, so, if you be not willing, there's no harm done. Perhaps you're shame-faced; some maidens, though they love a man well enough, yet they won't tell him so to his face. If that's the case, silence gives consent.

Prue

I'll speak sooner than you should believe that, and though one should always lie to a man, I'll speak the truth; I don't care—let my father do what he will; I'm too big to be whipped. So, I'll tell you plainly, I don't like you, nor love you at all, nor ever will. So there's your answer for you—and don't trouble me no more, you ugly thing!

Ben (angrily)

Look you, you woman—I spoke you fair, d'ye see, and

civil—as for your love and your liking, I don't value it more than a rope's end—in fact I like you as little as you do me. I tell you one thing, if you should give such words at sea, you'd have a cat o' nine tails laid across your shoulders. Fleah! Who are you? You heard the other handsome woman speak civilly to me—whatever you think of yourself, God, I don't compare you to her more than a bottle of beer to a bottle of port wine.

Prue

Well, and there's a handsome gentleman, and a fine gentleman, and a sweet gentleman that loves me, and I love him—and if he sees you speak to me any more, he'll thrash your jacket for you, he will, you great Sea-calf.

Ben

He'll eat salt for his supper for all that. What does Father mean to leave me alone as soon as I come home with such a dowdy? Sea-calf! I ain't calf enough to lick your painted face—you cheese curd you! Marry you! Oons, I'll sooner marry a Lapland witch!

Prue

I won't be called names, nor I won't be abused—no, I won't. If I were a man (bursting into tears) you durst not talk this way to me—no you durst not, you stinking tar barrel.

Ben

Tar barrel? Oons, let your pet fop say that to me!

Lady Foresight (entering)

Bless me, what's the matter? What does she cry for? Mr. Benjamin, what have you done to her?

Ben

Let her cry. The more she cries, the less she'll—she's been gathering foul weather in her mouth, and now it rains out at her eyes.

Lady Foresight

Come, Miss, come along with me, and tell me what the brute did, poor child.

Prue

Oh, Mother—I mean Laetitia—it was so awful—

ACT III
SCENE 6

The same, early evening.

Enter Ben and Mrs. Frail, whispering.

Ben

Father has nothing to do with me; why not tell him?

Mrs. Frail

My dear, we must keep it secret until your father settles the estate on you. He's a very passionate old man and very vengeful when thwarted. But you'll break my heart if you forsake me after all.

Ben

Break your heart! Why, I'd rather scuttle my ship. You don't think a sailor is false like a landsman?

Mrs. Frail

Will you always love me?

Ben

Once I love, I stick like pitch.

(They go out, still whispering. Enter Valentine and Scandal in close conversation.)

Valentine

Do allow Tattle to be a wit that you may see a fool.

Scandal

That's hard. What would you bring me to?

Valentine

I have noise and merriment to keep Lady Foresight's head from working. Hell is not more busy than her brain, nor contains more devils.

Scandal

I thought your fear of her had been over. She has failed in her project to make Foresight prevent Angelica from marrying you.

Valentine

True. Thanks to Angelica's willfulness. But she will try again unless diverted. None but you and Maskwell are acquainted with her passion for me. Ever since I first refused her, she has never given over trying to ruin me with Foresight, yet she had managed things so subtly that they have born the face of kindness.

Scandal

Exquisite woman! Does she think you have no more sense than to ruin yourself with Angelica by sleeping with her aunt?

Valentine

Lord knows what her idea is. Jack Maskwell has promised me to watch her closely.

Scandal

So you have manned your guard posts—but I hope you have not set your weakest guard where the enemy is strongest.

Valentine

You suspect Maskwell?

Scandal

I cannot help it. I am a little superstitious about faces like that.

Valentine

He owes me a great deal. It is through me that he gained the position of Foresight's secretary. Foresight is very close to him.

Scandal

With Lady Foresight you mean?

Valentine

Lady Foresight!

Scandal

There is some secret between them you do not suspect—notwithstanding her passion for you.

Valentine

Pooh! Nothing in the world but his design to help me. He endeavors to be high in her esteem that he may assist me.

Scandal

I shall be glad to be mistaken. But Lady Foresight is handsome, cunning and naturally wanton. Maskwell is flesh and blood. Faith, I've a taste for her myself.

Valentine

I mean you shall indulge it. Make love to her.

Scandal

With all my heart. Only a man of my refined tastes can truly appreciate a woman like Lady Foresight. I'll to her immediately.

Valentine

You will oblige me immensely. Keep her busy.

Scandal

I'll go now.

(Exit Scandal.)

Valentine

Godspeed.

(Enter Maskwell.)

Maskwell

What will the wickedness of this world come to?

Valentine

How now, Jack? What so full of contemplation that you run over?

Maskwell

I'm glad you're come. I've just left Lady Foresight.

Valentine

And having trusted you with her secrets you are villainously bent on discovering them all to me, ha?

Maskwell

I'm afraid my weakness leans that way. But I don't know whether, in honor, I can discover them all.

Valentine

No tragic design upon my person, I hope?

Maskwell

No, a comical design upon mine!

Valentine

I'm struck mute. Explain.

Maskwell

We have been bargaining about the rate of your ruin—and whereas pleasure is generally paid with mischief, what mischief I do is to be paid with pleasure. In short, the price of your ruin is to be paid with the person of—

Valentine

Of Angelica. You forgot you told me before.

Maskwell

No, no—as an earnest of that bargain, I am to have full and fair possession of the person of Lady Foresight.

Valentine

Foh! You jest.

Maskwell

By this light, I am serious. Tomorrow evening at eight she will receive me in her chamber.

Valentine

Why, the woman is possessed!

Maskwell

Well, will you go in my stead?

Valentine

Into a hot furnace sooner!

Maskwell

I suspect she'll prove hot enough. But it would be more to our purpose for you to go, than for me.

Valentine

What d'ye mean?

Maskwell

Mean! Not to disappoint the lady, surely.

Valentine

But—

Maskwell

She will be in your power if you go. But someone comes and I dare not stay. We will talk of this later.

(Exit Maskwell and enter Scandal.)

Scandal

Valentine, get out of the way. My Lady Foresight is coming, and I shall never succeed; but I made love a great while to no purpose.

Valentine

Why, what's the matter? She's convinced I don't love her.

Scandal

I can't get an answer from her that does not begin with her honor, or her virtue, or her religion or some such cant. Then, she has told me the whole history of Foresight's years of courtship.

Valentine

Did she not tell you at what a distance she keeps him? He has confessed to me, that but at certain times—that is, I suppose, when she thinks one of her lovers has made her pregnant—Foresight never has the privilege of a husband. I wonder he has not told you his grievances.

Scandal

Excessively foolish. But that which gives me most hopes of her is her telling me of the many temptations she has resisted.

Valentine

Now then you have her. Bragging to a man of temptations overcome is a woman's way of challenging a man to engage her more to the purpose. Here comes Foresight. I'm going.

(Exit Valentine. Enter Foresight.)

Foresight

Ah, Mr. Scandal, there you are. My wife was looking for you.

Scandal

You are blessed with such a fine lady, sir.

Foresight

Quite so. Quite so. I tell you, Mr. Scandal, if it were not for one thing I would think myself the happiest man in the world.

Scandal

What can that be, sir?

Foresight

It is a grief to me that I have no son.

Scandal

That might easily be remedied. Lady Foresight is a fine buxom woman—

Foresight

Indeed she is, Mr. Scandal.

Scandal

And I should not take you to be so old—

Foresight

No, no. That's not it. No, no. That's not it.

Scandal

No? Then, what can the matter be?

Foresight

You'll scarcely believe me when I tell you. My lady is so nice—so nice—that I don't believe she would touch a man for the world—at least above once or twice a year.

Scandal

That is a lamentable story. My lady must be told of it. This is an injury to mankind and all posterity—

Foresight

Would to heaven you would, Mr. Scandal. You are mightily in her favor.

Scandal

We must have a son some way or other. I'll look to it.

Foresight

I shall be mightily indebted to you if you can inflict it.

Scandal

I shall get you a whole bevy of brats. Leave that to me.

(Enter Lady Foresight.)

Foresight

Wife, wife—my Lady Foresight.

Lady Foresight (busy with a letter)

I'm busy. Truly, I wonder at your behavior to me in company.

Scandal

Madame, if your ladyship pleases, I would talk with you privately.

Foresight

I wish you good success. I wish you good success.

Scandal

You are too kind, Mr. Foresight.

Lady Foresight

Husband, will you go for a nap? It's past noon. Mr. Scandal, your servant.

Scandal

You keep to a schedule, madame.

Foresight

My dear, lend me your looking-glass.

Scandal

Lend it to him, madame. (Lady Foresight gives her husband the looking-glass) My passion for you is grown so violent that I am no longer master of myself.

Lady Foresight

Was there ever such impudence, to make love to me before my husband's face? (aside) I like this mightily. (aloud) I swear I'll tell him.

Scandal

Do. I'll die a martyr to my love for you. But come a little farther this way, and I'll tell you how we may get him out of the way.

(Scandal and Lady Foresight move off and whisper.)

Foresight

To her, Mr. Scandal, to her! Hmm, I'm a little pale.

Lady Foresight

Are you all right, husband?

Foresight

Hmm, I'm a little pale and my pulse is racing. (aside) I hope Mr. Scandal is doing his bit as he promised. Perhaps tonight. I feel a throbbing in my head just thinking about the joy of it.

Scandal

Your lady says your sleep has been unquiet of late.

Foresight

Very likely. Oh, my pulse is galloping.

Lady Foresight

Oh, mighty restless, but I was afraid to tell him so. He has been subject to talking and starting.

Scandal

And did not used to be so?

Lady Foresight

Never, never, till the last three nights; I cannot say that he as once broken my rest since we have been married.

Foresight

I will take a nap. (aside) And have such dreams. Such lascivious dreams. To her, Mr. Scandal. To her.

Scandal

Do so, Mr. Foresight, and say your prayers. They may be blessed with fruition. You look better than you did.

Foresight

Do you think so?

Scandal

Yes, yes. It will be over in a short while. If you go to bed now (aside to Foresight) I believe I shall do your business for you with your lady.

Foresight

I hope so. (fervently) I hope so. (aside) Egad, I am faint and my pulse is racing with expectation. If only the Moon holds, and Venus is in conjunction—then it may go well.

Scandal

I hope Mars and Venus will be in conjunction while your wife and I are together.

(Exit Foresight.)

Lady Foresight

Well, and what use do you hope to make of this business? You don't think you are ever likely to succeed in your design upon me?

Scandal

Faith, I do; I have a better opinion of you and myself than to despair.

Lady Foresight

Did you ever hear such a toad? Harkee, devil, do you think any woman honest?

Scandal

Yes, several very honest; they'll cheat at cards sometimes, but that's nothing.

Lady Foresight

Pshaw, but virtuous!

Scandal

There are some fools in the world; but most are ugly. You are too pretty to suffer from such a defect in character.

Lady Foresight

Oh, monstrous! What of conscience and honor?

Scandal

Why, as for honor, you have secured that by marrying the noble Foresight, thus creating a perpetual opportunity for pleasure.

Lady Foresight

An opportunity for pleasure!

Scandal

Yes, a husband. That takes care of honor. I shall take

care of conscience.

Lady Foresight

So, you think we are free to do as we please?

Scandal

I love to speak my mind.

Lady Foresight

Why, then, I'll speak my mind. As to this affair between you and me, I'll confess it does not displease me. Your person is well enough.

Scandal

I have no great opinion of myself, but I'm neither ugly nor a fool.

Lady Foresight

But you have a villainous character; you are a libertine in speech as well as practice.

Scandal

He that cries stop thief, is often the very thief himself.

Lady Foresight

It is more dangerous to talk of love to you than to grant another man the last favor.

Scandal

Do not believe it. The liberty I take with others never concerns myself. I am a juggler.

Lady Foresight

But such a universal juggler

Scandal

Faith, I'm sound.

Lady Foresight

I'll swear you're impudent.

Scandal

I'll swear you're handsome.

Lady Foresight

Pish, you'd tell me so, though you didn't believe it.

Scandal

And you'd think so, though I did not tell you so. And

now, I think we know each other pretty well.

Lady Foresight

You had best go to bed and dream, too. Like my husband.

Scandal

Faith, I have a good, lively imagination and can dream much to the purpose if I set about it.

Lady Foresight

I swear, Mr. Scandal, you are very alluring and say many fine things. With blushes I must own it, you have shaken, as I may say, the very foundation of my honor.

Scandal (aside)

Egad, I'll endeavor to make it shake indeed, madame. (aloud) You do me an injury—

Lady Foresight

If I escape your blandishments, I shall be proud as long as I live.

Scandal (aside)

What care I how you value yourself? (aloud) And despise me.

Lady Foresight

Never. Gratitude forbid.

Scandal

Your charming tongue pursues the victory of your eyes—while at your feet, your poor adorer dies—

Lady Foresight

I am not safe if I stay here to hear this—

Scandal

Oh, do not go. Why are you so bewitching? (aside) She'd best snap soon. I'm almost at the end of my cant.

Lady Foresight

I protest you have given me a palpitation of the heart.

Scandal

I can't outlive this night without your favor.

Lady Foresight

Sir, you have conquered. What marble heart could fail to yield? I dare swear every circumstance of me trembles. I surrender myself to your uncontrollable embraces.

CURTAIN

ACT IV
SCENE 7

Same as Act I, the next morning.

Foresight, Lady Foresight and Sir Sampson are talking. Enter Scandal.

Scandal

Bad news, bad news.

Sir Sampson

What's the matter?

Scandal

Undoubtedly, Mr. Foresight knew all this and might have prevented it.

Foresight

'Tis no earthquake! I only prevent earthquakes.

Scandal

No, no.

Sir Sampson

Why, body of me, out with it.

Scandal

Your son, Valentine, has been taken very ill. It's his wits. He speaks little, yet says he has a world to say. He says he has secrets to impart. I suppose to you, Mr. Foresight, and to you, Sir Sampson, for he calls you both. I can get nothing out of him. He desires to see you today, but would not be disturbed at present because he has some business in a dream.

Sir Sampson

Hoity-toity, what have I to do with his dreams? Body of me, this is a trick to get out of his contract. His solemn contract. No doubt the devil will tell him in a dream not to part with his inheritance. But I'll bring a parson to tell him the devil's a liar. If that won't do, I'll bring a lawyer that shall out-lie the devil.

Scandal

He's stark mad.

Sir Sampson

Mad. Some say from the barbarous usage he has received at your hands, and at the hands of his mistress, Angelica.

Foresight

What, is he non compos mentis?

Scandal

Quite non compos, sir.

Foresight

Why, then all's obliterated, Sir Sampson. If he's non compos mentis his act and deed will be of no effect. It's no good in law. I told you to consult me as to the time; I saw madness in his face.

Sir Sampson

Oons, I won't believe it; let me see him, sir. Mad. I'll make him find his senses.

Foresight

Saw it in his face.

Sir Sampson

Damn your predictions!

Foresight (offended)

The marriage is off. Your son is no match for my daughter. I'm a lawyer, and I'll tell you—the only ones who make anything out of a lawsuit are the lawyers. Besides, I won't force my girl; Prue wanted none of Mr. Benjamin anyway.

Sir Sampson

I shall run mad myself.

(Exit Sir Sampson in a fury.)

Foresight

Wherein was I mistaken, not to have foreseen this?

Scandal (to Lady Foresight)

Madame, you and I can tell him something else that he did not foresee.

Lady Foresight

What do you mean? I don't understand you.

Scandal

Hush—the pleasures of last night, my dear, too considerable to be forgot so soon.

Lady Foresight

Last night! Last night was the same as the night before, I think.

Scandal

S'death, do you make no difference between me and your husband?

Lady Foresight

Not much—he's superstitious and you are mad.

Scandal

You make me mad. You are not serious. Pray recollect yourself.

Lady Foresight

Oh, yes. Now, I remember. You were very impertinent and impudent—and would have come to bed with me?

Scandal

And did not?

Lady Foresight

Did not? With what face can you ask that question?

Scandal

This I have heard before, but never quite believed. The world says you can quite forget the man you have lain with all night—and deny favors done with more impudence than you can grant them.

Lady Foresight

It's a damned lying world.

Scandal

Madame, I'm your humble servant and honor you.

Foresight (to himself)

It's a great consolation to have a particular friend like Mr. Scandal. He's still trying to move my wife. Would that he might succeed. She's so nice. So very nice.

Scandal

You look pretty well, Mr. Foresight. How did you rest last night?

Foresight

Truly, Mr. Scandal, I was so—so moved last night—with—with dreams and—visions—that I remember little.

Scandal

'Twas a very forgetting night.

Foresight (aside to Scandal)

I thank you for your endeavors.

Scandal

The pleasure was all mine. I doubt not but she'll be persuaded and you'll be a father of a bouncing boy. (aside) She may choose to forget—but I forgot to take precautions and, dame me, I've made more bastards than any three gallants in this town.

Foresight

Will you be pleased to try again?

Scandal

Faith, no. I've shot my bolt. If I did not succeed, I have no taste to do it over.

(Enter Lord Froth.)

Lord Froth

Where is all the company?

Foresight

The company? I don't know but everything is topsy-turvy.

Lord Froth

What's the matter? Where's my wife?

Foresight

All turned topsy-turvy, sure as a gun.

Lord Froth

How do you mean? My wife?

Foresight

The strangest posture of affairs.

Lord Froth

What, my wife?

Foresight

No, no. I mean the family. Your lady's affairs may be in a very good posture. I saw her go in the garden—

down by the bushes with Mr. Tattle.

Lord Froth

In the bushes with Mr. Tattle? How, where, what to do?

Foresight

I suppose they had been laying their heads together.

Lord Froth

How?

Foresight

About poetry, I suppose; making couplets.

Lady Foresight

Oh, here they come now.

(Enter Lady Froth and Mr. Tattle.)

Tattle

My Lord, your humble servant. The finest day—

Lady Froth

My dear, Mr. Tattle and I have been star gazing, I don't know how long.

Foresight

Does it not tire your ladyship? Are you not weary of looking up?

Lady Froth

Oh, no. I love it violently—my dear, you're melancholy.

Lord Froth

No, my dear, I'm just awake.

Lady Froth

Sniff some of my hartshorn.

Lord Froth

I've some of my own, thank you, my dear.

Lady Froth

Well, Mr. Tattle, you understand astronomy like an almanac. Like a Greek.

Tattle

Not comparably to your ladyship.

Lady Froth

Shall you and I make an almanac together?

Tattle

With all my heart.

(Exit Lady Froth and Tattle followed by a suspicious Lord Froth. Enter Angelica in excitement.)

Angelica (agitated)

What's the matter with Valentine? I have heard he's ill.

Scandal

No strange matter, madame; he's mad, that's all.

Lady Foresight

I suppose you have thought him so a great while?

Angelica

All women think their lovers mad. Their love is certain proof if it. (troubled) How d'ye mean mad?

Scandal

Why, faith, madame, he's mad for want of his wits. His head is as light as his pockets.

Angelica

If you speak the truth, your endeavoring at wit is very

unseasonable.

Scandal

I had no idea his affliction would trouble you.

Angelica

You can't think me guilty of so much inhumanity as not to be concerned for a man I must own myself obliged to. May I see him?

Scandal

I'm afraid his physician is not willing you should see him yet.

Angelica

As you are his friend, I beseech you—

Scandal

Be not too much concerned, madame. I hope his condition is not desperate: an acknowledgement of love from you, perhaps, would work a cure.

Angelica (aside)

Is that how the land lies? (aloud) Acknowledgement of love! You mistake my compassion for a weakness I am a stranger to. If he can't be cured without my sucking the poison from the wound, I'm afraid he won't recover his senses until I lose mine.

Scandal

Won't you see him, then, if he desires it?

Angelica

What signifies a madman's desires? Besides, 'twould make me uneasy. If I don't see him, my concern for him will lessen. If I forget him, it's no more than he has done by himself.

Scandal

You were confessing just now an obligation to his love.

Angelica

But passions are unreasonable and involuntary; if he loves and it drives him mad, he can't help it—help it any more than I can help my want of inclination to stay here any longer.

(Angelica flounces out.)

Scandal (shaking his head)

An admirable composition, this same womankind.

Foresight

What, is she gone?

Scandal

Why, she was never here nor anywhere else; and I don't know her if I see her, nor do you.

Lady Foresight

This is some trick of Valentine's. Angelica sees it, too. Go forward with the marriage.

Foresight

No, the marriage is definitely off. Prue doesn't like Mr. Ben and I won't force her.

ACT IV
SCENE 8

The scene changes to Valentine's room. He lies disheveled on a couch.

Enter Angelica, escorted by Scandal.

Angelica

Do you know me, Valentine?

Valentine (starting up)

Oh, very well.

Angelica

Who am I?

Valentine

You are woman. The reflection of heaven in a pond—he that leaps in you is—sunk. I know you; for I loved a woman—and I loved her so long that I found out what a woman is good for.

Angelica

What's that?

Valentine

Why, to keep a secret.

Angelica

Oh, Lord, stark mad.

Valentine

Oh, exceedingly good to keep a secret: for though she should tell, yet she is not to be believed.

Scandal

I'll leave you together.

Angelica

Oh, heavens, you won't leave me alone with a madman?

Scandal

No, madame, I only leave a madman to his remedy.

Valentine

Madame, you need not be very much afraid, for I fancy I begin to come to myself.

(Exit Scandal.)

Angelica (aside)

I'll be hanged if I don't make you stark mad in good earnest before I'm through.

Valentine

You see what love brings us to. Now let us understand one another.

Angelica

Heaven knows I pity you. Could I have foreseen the effects, I would have tried to love you, but it's too late.

Valentine

What's too late? I am not mad.

Angelica (aside)

You shall be. (aloud) Is it a trick then?

Valentine

Yes, to deceive my father.

Angelica

And I thought your love to me had caused this delirium.

(sadly) How disappointing. I nearly came to love you.

Valentine

Nearly! Oh, barbarous!

(Scandal returns.)

Angelica

So, you did this not for love, but only for mercenary ends?

Valentine

Now you do me wrong.

Angelica

Perhaps you thought me mercenary. But how am I deluded by this interval of sense to reason with a madman.

Valentine

I am not mad.

Angelica

Oh, here's a reasonable creature. Scandal, acknowledge the trick; confess the madness is counterfeit.

Scandal

Counterfeit, Madame? I'll maintain him to be as absolutely and substantially mad as any Chemist, Lover or Poet in Europe.

Valentine

S'death, you lie. I am not mad.

Angelica

Ha, ha, ha, you see, he denies it.

Scandal

Did you ever know a madman who didn't?

Valentine

'Tis time to stop the jest.

Scandal

Why, yes, he has intervals. But see how wild he looks now.

Valentine

This farce is done. I will be mad no longer.

Angelica

Ha, ha, ha. Is he mad or not?

Scandal

Certainly, for he does not know his own mind for two minutes. Sir, your father is below and asks for you. That's why I returned. Will you be mad or not?

Valentine

Mad, of course. I will be mad to everybody but this lady.

Scandal

Just so. Shall I permit him to come up?

Valentine

Let him wait.

Angelica

Oh, by no means. I'm going.

Valentine

Will you leave me in this uncertainty?

Angelica

Would anyone but a madman complain of uncertainty? Uncertainty and Expectation are the joys of life. Security is a dull, insipid thing. I am not the fool you take me for; and you are mad and don't know it. Adieu.

(Angelica exits.)

Valentine

From a riddle you can expect nothing but a riddle.

Scandal

I hear your father's step. Back to your couch.

(Valentine leaps to the couch and disarranges his hair, looks wild.)

Valentine

Ha, what's that?

(Enter Sir Sampson, somewhat timidly for him.)

Scandal

For heaven's sake, softly and gently; don't provoke him.

Valentine

Answer me; who is that?

Sir Sampson

Egad, does he not know me? I'll speak gently. Val, Val—do you know me, boy? What, not know your own father?

Valentine

It may be so. I had a father once. I did not know you—the world is full—there are people that we know and people that we don't know; and—and yet (softly) the sun shines on all alike. There are fathers that have many children, and children that have many fathers—strange—BUT I AM TRUTH AND COME TO GIVE THE WORLD THE LIE!

Sir Sampson

This is strange.

Valentine

Why do you wear black? Do you wear your conscience on your outside? Do you know me?

Sir Sampson

Yes.

Valentine

You lie, for I am truth. But, I'll tell you one thing; it's a question that would puzzle a mathematician—whether the Bible saves more souls in Westminster Abbey or damages more souls in Westminster Hall? For my part, I am truth and cannot tell. I have very few acquaintances.

Sir Sampson

He's babbling—does he have intervals?

Scandal

Very few.

Valentine

'Tis well. What o'clock is it? My father here? Your blessing, sir.

Sir Sampson

Bless thee, Val. How are you, boy?

Valentine (jubilant)

Pretty well, sir. Won't you please sit down?

Sir Sampson

I will. Come, boy, you shall sit down by me.

Valentine

That were disrespectful.

Sir Sampson

No, no. Come, sit thee down. Let me feel your pulse. Pretty well. I'm glad you are better, honest Val.

Valentine

Thank you, Dad.

Sir Sampson

Your hand does not shake. I believe you can write, Val, ha, boy? Can you write your name, Val? Come, show your father what you can do.

(Valentine doesn't respond.)

Sir Sampson

Do you know this paper, Val? (showing a paper, but holding it beyond Valentine's reach)

Valentine

I can't tell. Let me see.

Sir Sampson

See it, boy? Why, you see it there. It's your own hand. Let me see, I can read it as plain as can be. Look you here: (reading) "The condition of this obligation—" And then, at the bottom: "As witness my hand, Valentine Plyant": in great letters. Why it's as plain as can be. I believe I can read it farther off yet.

(Sir Sampson stretches his arm out as long as he can.)

Valentine

May I hold it, sir?

Sir Sampson

Hold it? Why, with all my heart? But, what need anybody to hold it? I'll put it in my pocket and then nobody need hold it. There, Val, safe enough.

Valentine

What? Who are you?

Sir Sampson

Eh, don't you know me?

Valentine

Is my bad genius here again? No, it is a devil with an itching palm; and he's come to be scratched. My nails are not long enough. Let me have a pair of red hot tongs, then you shall see me lead the devil by the nose.

Sir Sampson

Lord, Lord. I'll not venture myself with a madman.

Valentine

Who's that talks out of his way? I am truth and can set him right. Harkee, friend, the straight road is the worst you can go. He that follows his nose, often will be led to a stink.

Sir Sampson

What the devil had I to do, ever to beget sons? Why did I ever marry?

Valentine

Because you were a monster, old boy. The two greatest monsters in the world are a man and a woman. What's thy opinion?

Sir Sampson

Why, my opinion is that these two joined together

make yet a greater— a man and his wife.

Valentine

Ha, old true penny, do you say so? But, it's wonderful strange.

Sir Sampson

What is?

Valentine

That grey hairs should cover a green head and I make a fool of my father.

(Enter Foresight.)

Foresight

What does he say? Has he uttered any prophecies or oracles?

Sir Sampson

A pox on your prognostications. Oons, that you could not foresee that the moon would predominate and my son run mad.

Foresight

But, I did, Brother, I did. Did I not say I saw madness

in his face?

(Exit Sir Sampson in a rage.)

Sir Sampson

You're a fool; he's a fool; we're all fools.

Foresight

It's really a pity that man is so ignorant.

ACT IV
SCENE 9

Same as Act I.

Enter Benjamin and Mrs. Frail.

Ben

All mad, I think—all the monsters of the deep are come ashore.

Mrs. Frail

Mr. Benjamin in a rage?

Ben

No, I'm pleased well enough now I have found you. I have weathered such a hurricane on your account.

Mrs. Frail

My account, what's the matter?

Ben

Why, Father found me squabbling with that chitty-faced thing he would have me marry. I told him in plain terms if I were minded to marry, I'd marry to please myself—not him. As to the young woman he provided for me, I think it more fitting she should be learning her copy book and making dirt pies than looking for a husband. I have another voyage to make.

Mrs. Frail

Do you intend to go to sea again?

Ben.

No, no—my mind runs on you—but I did not tell him so much. Then he told me the match was off anyway because brother Val is gone mad. I was sorry to hear Val is sick o the head, but it's an ill wind that blows no one any good, as the saying is.

Mrs. Frail

Then why are you so upset?

Ben

Because now Father will have me marry that flighty thing Angelica.

Mrs. Frail

Angelica?

Ben

She's a fine woman, but she flies too high for this poor sailor. I would not be led around by the nose like my brother Val. I told him I would not venture in that direction.

Mrs. Frail

Why, what happened then?

Ben

He became more angry than a Northwester. He said he'd marry her himself if I didn't.

Mrs. Frail

Sir Sampson marry Angelica?

Ben

I told him if he played the fool and married at these years there was more danger of his head aching than my heart. He hadn't a word to say but that he'd disinherit me if I didn't pay my addresses to Angelica.

Mrs. Frail

Well then, you must obey him.

Ben

Obey him? I want to marry you. Sure, you're mad, too.

Mrs. Frail

If you want to marry me, you must learn to do as I say—and in this case, obey your father.

Ben

I can't see why.

Mrs. Frail

Let me manage this. Have no fear, Angelica will reject you. She loves Valentine.

Ben

He's welcome to that one. But, around that woman—I—I'm tongue-tied, as it were—

Mrs. Frail

So much the better, you're sure to fail and that insures success.

Ben

Eh?

(Enter Angelica, reading a book.)

Mrs. Frail

Oh, Ben. You are come at a critical moment. Here's Angelica. Pursue your point, now or never.

Ben.

I would gladly have been encouraged with a bottle or two—

Mrs. Frail

Foh, a drunken lover. There's no time for that.

Ben

But, I shall break my mind—that is, upon further acquaintance. (approaching Angelica, who continues reading) So, for the present, I'll take my leave. (Ben retreats) You'll make my excuse.

Mrs. Frail

What? You must not be daunted.

Ben

Daunted. No, no. If I set on it, I'll do it. But, for the present—till further acquaintance— (leaving)

Mrs. Frail

You'll never lose such a favorable opportunity if I can help it. I'll leave you together and lock the door.

(Exit Mrs. Frail, locking the door.)

Ben

No, no. I've forgotten my gloves. (desperate) What d'ye do? Mrs. Frail, open the door. What a trick this is! Now she has seen me. (to Angelica, who ignores him) I made bold to pass through. (struggling with the door) I think this door's enchanted.

Angelica (declaiming)

Spare me, gentle boy, Press me no more For that slight toy—

Ben

Eh. Cousin, your servant.

Angelica

Mr. Benjamin.

Ben

No offense, I hope.

Angelica

Have you any business with me?

Ben

Not at present. I made bold to come and see if you were disposed to walk this evening?

Angelica

A walk? What then?

Ben

Nothing—only for the walk's sake.

Angelica

I nauseate walking. It's a country diversion. I loathe the country.

Ben

Do you? Well, perhaps a play?

Angelica

I hate the town, too.

Ben

Hate them both. 'Tis like you may.

Angelica

Ha, ha, ha. Yes, 'tis like I may. You have nothing more to say to me?

Ben

Not at present.

Angelica

I have a little business, if you will excuse me.

Ben

When you are deposed, when you are deposed. Now's as well as another time; another time's as well as now. There's no haste. It will keep cold as they say. Cousin, your servant. I think this door is locked.

Angelica

You may go this way.

(Angelica points to another door and Ben dashes for it.)

Ben

By your leave.

Angelica

Ha, ha, ha.

(Angelica waits, then follows Ben out. After a pause, Lord Froth and Tattle enter.)

Tattle

Your Lordship is so merry.

Froth

Merry. O barbarous. I'd as soon you called me a fool.

Tattle

But your laughter is so becoming.

Froth

Ridiculous. I laugh at nobody's jest but my own, or a lady's—I assure you.

Tattle

Let me perish. Do I never say anything worthy of laughter?

Froth

Don't misapprehend me. I often smile at you. But there is nothing so unfashionable as to laugh—everybody can laugh—even a peasant. Now then, when I laugh, I always laugh alone.

Tattle

That's because you laugh at your own jests.

Froth

Your raillery provokes me to a smile.

Tattle (looking in his mirror)

Deuce take me, I have encouraged a pimple.

Froth

Then you must mortify him with a patch. My wife will supply you. I see her coming.

(Enter Lady Froth.)

Lady Froth

Ah, Parnassus. Mr. Tattle, I have the most exquisite simile to show you.

Tattle

With all my heart.

(Lady Froth exits with Mr. Tattle, leaving a vexed Lord Froth by himself.)

Froth

Is it come to this?

(Enter Prue.)

Prue

Oh, Lord Froth, I'm glad you are here. I have been looking up and down for you like anything.

Froth (coldly)

Indeed, my dear.

Prue

Oh, I have wonderful news—wonderful news. I must not marry that sea porpoise, my father says so.

Froth

I'm glad you are so happy, child, to lose a husband.

Prue

But now I can marry you.

Froth

Who told you that, child?

Prue

Why you did—you said you loved me.

Froth

But that was yesterday, child. I slept a whole night and did not so much as dream of the matter. Besides I'm already married.

Prue

But can't you divorce her, or send her away?

Froth

No, no. (aside) Though if I did, it would not be for such a chit as this. (aloud) Divorce is too unfashionable. It's only for common people. Fie, you're a woman now and must think of a new man every evening. No, child, you would not have me—

Prue

No? But, I would, though—

Froth

You forget you're a woman and don't know your down mind. Better run play with your dolls, child.

(Exit Froth.)

Prue

AWW. HOO, HOO, HOO.

(Prue bawls and falls into a tantrum, jumps up and down, rolls on the floor and beats her heels.

(Enter Foresight.)

Foresight

Mercy on us. What do these lunacies portend? Are you mad, child?

Prue

I WANT A HUSBAND!

Foresight

You just refused Mr. Benjamin?

Prue

I want a husband, not a sea monster. What, must I be a child forever and sleep with nurse? Indeed, I won't. I will have a man someway or other. Oh, when I think about a man, I feel hot and shivery inside— oh—

Foresight

This lunacy is catching. Hussy, you shall have the rod.

Prue

A fiddle for a rod. The only rod I want is a husband. If you don't get me one, I'll get one for myself. Mr. Maskwell says he loves me, and he's a handsome man.

Foresight

Did he so? Rogue. Nurse, Nurse!

(Enter Nurse.)

Nurse

Yes, sir?

Foresight

Take Miss to her room and lock her up. And then, tell that villain Maskwell to make ready his accounts. He leaves this house tonight.

(Nurse exits, wrestling with a screaming Prue.)

Foresight

All mad, all mad. Surely the nation is endangered. These portents can signify nothing less than a national catastrophe. Yes, it must be—the French will invade—I'd better warn the countryside.

(Enter Sir Sampson and Angelica.)

Sir Sampson

Where is the Old Soothsayer? This uncle of mine elect? Aha, Old Copernicus, Uncle Foresight, wish me joy, double joy, both as uncle and astrologer. Here's a conjunction that was not foretold in all your zodiacs. You're an old fellow, Foresight, I mean Uncle Foresight—and yet you shall dance at my wedding. We'll have the music of the spheres for thee, Old Ptolemy, that we will.

Foresight

You are not married to my niece?

Sir Sampson

Not absolutely married, Uncle, but very near it, within a kiss, you see.

Angelica

Very true, indeed, Uncle. I hope you'll be my father and give me away.

Sir Sampson

That he shall, or I'll burn his globes and zodiacs. He shall be your father, and you shall make me a father, and I'll make you a mother.

Foresight

This is so surprising.

Sir Sampson

Surprising, Uncle? Not at all. It's a plot to undermine cold weather.

(Enter Lady Foresight and Ben.)

Lady Foresight

I'm glad to hear there's so much fire in you, Sir Sampson.

Ben

I fear his fire's little better than tinder; it will only serve to light a candle for someone else.

Sir Sampson (in a rage)

Who gave you authority to speak in this case? To your element, fish— rule your own helm, don't direct me.

Ben

Take care of your own helm, or you won't keep her under sail for long.

Sir Sampson

You impudent tarpaulin. Do you bring your filthy forecastle jests upon your father?

Lady Foresight

Out upon it—at years of discretion and conduct yourself at this rate.

Ben

No offense, Aunt.

Lady Foresight

No offense? As I'm a person, I'm ashamed of you. Foh, how you stink of wine. Do you think my daughter will ever endure such a tankard? You're an absolute tankard.

Ben

Tankard? If you grudge me liquor, make up a bill. Give me more drink, and take my purse. (singing) Prithee, fill me the glass, He that whines for a lass, Is an ignorant ass. (stops singing) But if you would have me marry my cousin, say the word, and I'll do it. Ben will do it. That's the word. Ben will do it, that's my crest—my motto, I have forgot.

Lady Foresight

Ben is a little drunk from drinking your health, Angelica.

Ben

In vino veritas, Aunt. I have drunk your health today, Cousin. I am a tankard. But if you have a mind to be married, say the word, Ben will do it. If she has her maidenhead, let her look to it. Ben will do it. If she has not, let her cry out, at nine months' end: "Ben did it."

Angelica

Your pardon, Aunt, I can stay no longer. Cousin Ben grows very powerful—egh, how he smells. I shall be overcome with the fumes if I stay.

Lady Foresight

Smells? He would poison an apothecary and his family.

I don't know what to do with him. You are not fit to live in a Christian Commonwealth. Go to the Saracens, or the Tartars, or the Turks—beastly pagan.

Ben

Turks, no; no Turks, Aunt. Your Turks are infidels and believe not in the grape. My map says your Turk is not orthodox. It is a plain case, that Orthodox is a hard word, Aunt, and (hiccup) Greek for Claret. (sings) To drink is a Christian diversion, Unknown to the Turk or the Persian, Let Mohammedan fools Live by heathenish rules, But let British lads sing: "A health to the King!" Hurrah.

Lady Foresight

Go lie down and sleep, you sot, or as I'm a person, I'll have you beaten with broomsticks. Call up the wenches with broomsticks.

Ben

Ahoy. Wenches, where are the wenches?

(Enter Scandal.)

Lady Foresight

Dear Mr. Scandal, get him away. I have an affair that invades me with some precipitation—

Scandal

Come, brave sailor. Will you go to a cock fight?

Ben

With a wench? Is she a shake-bag? Lead on, Macbeth, lead on. Ben will do it. (singing) Let Mohammedan fools live by heathenish rules—

ACT IV
SCENE 10

Same as Act I, a little later.

Enter Foresight and Maskwell.

Foresight

Have you deceived me, you villain, and betrayed all the kindnesses you have received at my hands by paying addresses to my daughter?

Maskwell

Only to serve your honor.

Foresight

To serve me? How?

Maskwell

I thought a certain person was too much in her good graces and sought to act as a counterweight to prevent her from committing some folly.

Foresight

Who? Who dared to address my daughter without my consent?

Maskwell

I am loathe to say. Friendship binds me to silence. But he aims there no longer—be at ease on that account.

Foresight

Be easy? Where does he aim now?

Maskwell

At your wife.

Foresight

What?

Maskwell

I am sorry I can't make you an answer, this is an occasion on which I would not willingly be silent—but—

Foresight

If he is your friend, what am I?

Maskwell

I am answered.

Foresight

What is the villain's purpose?

Maskwell

I should rather give you an opportunity to observe than to speak ill of him—you know I mean Valentine.

Foresight

Nobly spoken.

Maskwell

If you will follow me to my Lady's chamber—

Foresight

Hell, I will.

Maskwell

Duty to you makes me do a severe justice. When everything is ready, I shall call you.

Foresight

By all the stars, I am your friend forever.

(Exit Foresight and Maskwell. Enter Scandal and Tattle, followed by Ben.)

Ben

Boys, boys, lads, where are you? Scandal, this is your trick—you're always spoiling company by leaving it.

Scandal

And you're always spoiling company by coming into it.

Ben

Pooh. Man, when I say you spoil company by leaving it, I mean you leave nobody for the company to laugh at. I think I was with you, ha?

Tattle

Most definitely.

Ben

Tell me more, Mr. Tattle, about my Aunt's reputation.

Tattle

More? Why I know nothing. Have I said anything about her reputation? Oh, fie.

Scandal

Mr. Tattle has a great reputation for secrecy.

Tattle

I thank heaven it has always been a part of my character to handle the reputation of others very tenderly.

Scandal

Such reputations as you have to deal with are in need of tender handling.

Tattle

How can you say that when you know not the persons of whom you speak?

Scandal

Not know them? Why, you never had to do with anybody that did not stink to all the town.

Tattle

As I hope to be saved, I never exposed a woman since I knew what a woman was. I never could meddle with a woman that had to do with anybody else.

Ben

How?

Scandal

Except her husband, Tattle.

Tattle

Oh, that.

Scandal

Yet, you were once fond of Mrs. Frail.

Ben (aside)

What's this?

Tattle

Till I found out her intrigue with Valentine. Oh, what have I said? My unlucky tongue.

Scandal

Ha, ha, ha.

Ben

Mrs. Frail?

Scandal

Yes, Mrs. Frail is a very fine woman. We all know her.

Tattle

Oh, that is not fair.

Scandal

What?

Tattle

To tell.

Scandal

To tell what? What do I know of Mrs. Frail? I don't know if she is a man or woman—except by her dress.

Tattle

No?

Scandal

No.

Tattle

She says otherwise.

Scandal

Impossible.

Tattle

Ask Valentine.

Scandal

Why, then I believe a woman only obliges a man that she may have the pleasure of telling herself.

Tattle

No doubt on it? Well, but has she done you wrong or not? You have had her?

Scandal

I have more honor than to tell first, but I have never contradicted a lady in my life.

Ben

Then you own it?

Scandal

I can't deny it if she says so.

Ben

Mayhap, I'll ask her.

Scandal

Barbarous. Ask a lady?

Ben (aside)

This is lucky. I was about to marry my brother's whore. Nay, everybody's whore.

Scandal

Come, let us go back to the company. Mum's the word as to all this. No harm done—all friends here.

CURTAIN

ACT V
SCENE 11

Lady Foresight's Bed Chamber, a little later that evening.

Lady Foresight is pacing impatiently, playing with her fan. Enter Maskwell.

Lady Foresight

You are late. I was accusing you of neglect.

Maskwell

Excess of joy has made me stupid.

Lady Foresight

You can excuse a fault too well, a ready answer shows you were prepared.

Maskwell

Guilt is at a loss; innocence never—

Lady Foresight

Not in love—love has no language to be heard—

Maskwell

Who would not lose speech to have your favors? (kisses her)

Lady Foresight

Let me lock the door first, so that it's safe.

(Valentine steps from behind the curtains.)

Valentine

And may all treachery be thus discovered.

Lady Foresight

AHHH!

Maskwell (running out)

Fortunately, I have provided an escape for myself.

Valentine

Hold, madame, hold. You have no more holes to your burrow. I'll stand between you and this sally port.

Lady Foresight

Thunder will strike thee dead.

Valentine

Be patient.

Lady Foresight

Be damned.

Valentine

Consider, I have you on the hook.

Lady Foresight

I'll hold my breath and die, but I'll be free.

(Maskwell returns, leading in Angelica and Foresight.)

Maskwell (whispering to Foresight)

I have kept my word. He's here best discovered.

(Maskwell leaves.)

Maskwell

I will not be seen in this.

Foresight

Hell and—she's in tears.

Lady Foresight (low to Valentine)

If I repent? You will not expose me?

Valentine

I will be your friend in every honest way.

Lady Foresight (seeing her husband and Angelica, aside)

Witnesses. Then all's my own. (aloud, dropping to her knees) Never, never—kill me—I'll die before I consent to such a sin—

Valentine

Ha.

Lady Foresight

Cruel man, I'll forgive all you've done. And I won't tell. Do not ravish me.

Foresight

Monster! Dog! I'm old, but by the stars, I'll fight.

(Foresight rushes at Valentine with his cane. Angelica and Lady Foresight restrain him.)

Angelica

Hold, hold.

Valentine

Sorceress.

Lady Foresight (to Foresight)

Moderate your passion. He's mad, alas, he's mad.

Foresight

You excuse him?

Lady Foresight

Indeed, he is, my Lord, and knows not what he does. See how wild he looks.

Valentine

By heaven, 'twere senseless not to be mad and see such witchcraft.

Lady Foresight

You hear him? He talks idly.

Valentine

Now, by my soul, I will not go till I have made known my wrongs—and yours—though she has the hosts of hell as her servants.

Lady Foresight

Alas, he raves. Talks poetry. For heaven's sake, husband, come away before he attempts some extravagance.

Valentine

Angelica, will you hear me?

(Angelica turns her back on him and stalks out.)

Valentine (to Foresight)

Will you not hear me? Why, by heaven, she laughs, grins, points to your back; she forks out cuckoldom with her fingers—and you're not running horn mad after your future.

(Lady Foresight turns and smiles at Valentine as she and Foresight leave.)

Foresight

He's mad, indeed. I'll send Maskwell to him.

Lady Foresight

I'll faint if I stay.

ACT V
SCENE 12

Same as Act I, later that night.

Ben enters and lies down on a couch out of sight. Enter Maskwell and Lady Foresight.

Maskwell

Was it not lucky?

Lady Foresight

Lucky? It might have been my ruin.

Maskwell

But fortune is your own.

Lady Foresight

Not yet. The honey-tongued devil has somehow persuaded Angelica that it was all a mistake. How, I do not know.

Maskwell

They are coming now; best not be seen together.

(Exit Lady Foresight.)

Maskwell (aside)

So it takes. Angelica believes Valentine because I told her the whole plot. Valentine trusts me absolutely now; so now is the time to line my own pockets.

Valentine

Ah, dear Maskwell. But for your good words, this lady would never have even spoken to me.

Maskwell

Despite what's happened, all can be saved yet.

Angelica

My uncle is being very troublesome. He will do everything he can to prevent the marriage and, while he cannot succeed, now that I have made up my mind, he can cause a lot of trouble.

Maskwell

It must be by elopement. It is vain to talk anymore.

Angelica

An elopement? How very common.

Valentine

He's right. I know no other way—if you have love enough to run this venture?

Angelica

Love enough? I don't know that—but I have obstinacy enough to oppose anything that resists my will though it were reason itself.

Valentine (aside)

Egad, frank at least.

Maskwell

I'll secure the proper papers and run the hazard with you.

Angelica

But how can we escape without suspicion?

Maskwell

Leave that to my care. The coach shall be got ready by your uncle's own order.

Valentine

How?

Maskwell

I will tell him the whole of the contrivance. That's my way.

Valentine

How will that help?

Maskwell

Why, I will tell my Lord I laid this plot with you on purpose to betray you—and that while she thinks she is marrying you, she will actually be marrying Sir Sampson.

Valentine

So?

Maskwell

So, while you're busy getting ready, Sir Sampson will whisk her away.

Valentine

I see. You'll tell him that.

Maskwell

Yes. Why, don't you think I mean to do so?

Valentine

No, no. I dare swear you will not. Excellent Maskwell, you were certainly meant to be a statesman—but you are too honest.

Maskwell

Well, get yourself ready. Go by the back stairs. We'll meet here in an hour.

(Exit Valentine with a gesture of admiration for his friend. Ben's head appears over the top of the sofa and then disappears.)

Ben (aside)

Do you say so?

Maskwell

Madame, will you be ready?

Angelica

For once in my life, I will be punctual.

Maskwell

Stay. Upon second thought, we had best meet in my chamber. It will be more convenient.

Angelica

I am guided by you, but Valentine will mistake.

Maskwell

No, I'll tell him straightaway.

Angelica

I will not fail.

(Exit Angelica.)

Maskwell

'Tis no fault of mine. I have told them in plain terms how easy it is to cheat them; and if they will not hear the serpent's hiss, they must be stung, now to—

(Ben rises up with a pistol in his hand.)

Maskwell

What the devil?

Ben

Ahoy there!

Maskwell

What do you mean by this rudeness?

Ben

D'ye see, I've been dozing her and heard all your plan. I understand your trick, my little shark.

Maskwell

Will you expose me?

Ben

No, I mean to profit by it.

Maskwell

What do you mean?

Ben

That you don't need to concern yourself with, little shark. If you'll just accompany me to a closet, I shall secure your cooperation.

ACT V
SCENE 13

Same as Act I.

Foresight, Mrs. Foresight, Lord Froth, Lady Froth are playing at cards. Tattle and Scandal are also present.

Enter Sir Sampson and Mrs. Frail.

Sir Sampson

Brother, the most unlucky accident.

Foresight

What's the matter?

Sir Sampson

Oh, the two most unfortunate creatures.

Lady Foresight

Bless us, how so?

Sir Sampson

Mrs. Frail and I are— Oons, I can't speak it out.

Mrs. Frail

Married.

Lady Foresight

Married? How?

Sir Sampson

Ben did it. But this is the most cruel thing. To marry someone one does not know. Body o me if I ever was concerned like this in my life. It was a trick, I thought it was Angelica.

Lady Foresight

This is very unfortunate if you don't care for one another.

Sir Sampson

I never liked anybody less in my life. Poor woman. Gad, I'm sorry for her, too; for I have no reason to hate her neither; but I believe I shall lead her a damned sort of life.

Lady Foresight

He's better than no husband at all, I suppose. But mine's worth two on him.

Mrs. Frail

It's well it was no worse. It was Ben's idea. For my part, I always despised Sir Sampson of all things; nothing but his being my husband could make me like him less.

Sir Sampson

I thought as much. If only it could be kept secret.

Scandal

You'll agree very well in a little time; Custom will make it easy to you.

Sir Sampson

Easy! Damnation, I don't think I shall sleep tonight.

Mrs. Frail

Depend upon it, you shall not. What on your wedding night? You shall do your duty, Sir Sampson. We shall see if you are worthy of your name.

(Sir Sampson looks frightened.)

Sir Sampson

Argh.

Foresight

But, how did this come about?

Sir Sampson

I designed to marry Angelica privately—and she planned to cheat me by marrying Valentine. But somehow Ben cheated us both, substituted himself for Valentine and this lady for Angelica.

Lady Foresight

Ben married to Angelica! Then I am revenged.

Ben (haling in Angelica)

Give us joy.

Angelica

You brute. Beastly creature. I won't be married to you.

Ben

Married and consummated. That's good in law.

Angelica

But I thought you were Valentine.

Ben

You were not so unkind but a few moments ago.

Sir Sampson

Dog—do you trick your father and your brother?

Ben

And did you not mean to trick me? First, you would have me marry that little chit? Then you would put Mrs. Frail upon me, who was Valentine's mistress for several years? Did you think this old sea dog was a complete fool? (to Angelica) You, my lady should be thankful you are married to a gentleman and not to Maskwell. You, Father, are married to a very worthy lady who desired to be nearer related to you. What, you would not have your son marry a whore? She planned to marry Valentine. Why fooling you all is easier than standing a night's watch. As for you, young Mistress Weathervane, you shan't lead me the dance you led my brother, for at the first sign, I'll put to sea—d'ye conceive me? And if you do not behave on the voyage, I'll drown you like a cat.

Angelica

Inhuman monster. (aside) I begin to like him immensely.

Lady Foresight

Then I am revenged. Maskwell dares not speak and Valentine is ruined.

(Enter Valentine.)

Valentine

Brother, what have you done?

Ben

Only as you would have done by me.

Valentine

You'll answer for this.

Ben

Anytime. You know I am a better swordsman, Val. Better think twice.

Valentine

I'll pay you back.

Sir Sampson

Never mind, Val, what's done is done and cannot be undone. I'll be revenged on Ben, at least; I release you, Valentine, from your obligations. Come, comfort your father. Ben shall have none of my money.

Valentine

Sir, you oblige me much, and do a long way to reconciling myself to my loss of Angelica.

Ben

Forget her, Val. This jade wants a stronger hand than yours to control her. To love her is to be lost.

Angelica

Say you so, Porpoise? In a week, you shall be at my feet.

Valentine

It's true she has not been very kind.

Lady Foresight (aside)

Are they to be reconciled? Then, what of my revenge? (she tears her fan)

Scandal

From hence, let those be warned who mean to wed, lest mutual falsehood stain the marriage bed. For each deceiver to his cost my find that marriage frauds are often paid in kind.

CURTAIN

ABOUT THE AUTHOR

Frank J. Morlock has written and translated many plays since retiring from the legal profession in 1992. His translations have also appeared on Project Gutenberg, the Alexandre Dumas Père web page, Literature in the Age of Napoléon, Infinite Artistries.com, and Munsey's (formerly Blackmask). In 2006 he received an award from the North American Jules Verne Society for his translations of Verne's plays. He lives and works in México.